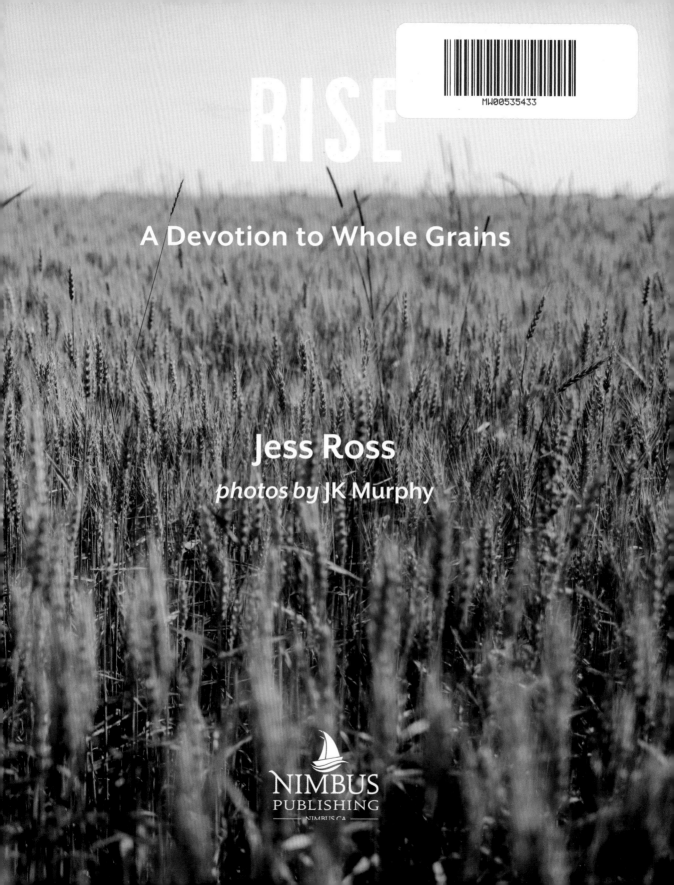

RISE

A Devotion to Whole Grains

Jess Ross

photos by JK Murphy

NIMBUS PUBLISHING
NIMBUS.CA

Nimbus Publishing Limited
3660 Strawberry Hill Street, Halifax, NS, B3K 5A9
(902) 455-4286 nimbus.ca

Nimbus Publishing is based in Kjipuktuk, Mi'kma'ki, the traditional territory of the Mi'kmaq People.

Editor: Simon Thibault
Editor for the press: Whitney Moran
Cover design: Heather Bryan
Graphic design and typesetting: Peggy & Co. Design

NB1547

Library and Archives Canada Cataloguing in Publication

Title: Rise : a devotion to whole grains / Jess Ross ; photos by JK Murphy.
Names: Ross, Jess, author. | Murphy, JK, photographer.
Description: Includes index.
Identifiers: Canadiana (print) 20230590926 | Canadiana (ebook) 20230590934 | ISBN 9781774712641 (softcover) | ISBN 9781774712832 (EPUB)
Subjects: LCSH: Cooking (Cereals) | LCSH: Grain. | LCSH: Baking. | LCSH: Baked products. | LCGFT: Cookbooks.
Classification: LCC TX808 .R67 2024 | DDC 641.6/31—dc23

Nimbus Publishing acknowledges the financial support for its publishing activities from the Government of Canada, the Canada Council for the Arts, and from the Province of Nova Scotia. We are pleased to work in partnership with the Province of Nova Scotia to develop and promote our creative industries for the benefit of all Nova Scotians.

This book was created on the lands of the Mi'kmaq, the Peskotomuhkati, and in Tkaronto on the land of the Mississaugas of the Credit, the Anishnabeg, the Chippewa, the Haudenosaunee, and the Wendat Peoples. As an uninvited guest and settler, I am committed to upholding the Peace and Friendship Treaties that govern this land as best I can. Working toward a sustainable, grain sovereign future is one way I honour the land and move towards liberation.

I dedicate this book to Gen Z. I'm deeply inspired and motivated by the brilliance and power of this generation. I'll do all that I can with my elder millennial zeal to work towards a society for you that deeply values life on earth and where everyone eats really well.

—JR

CONTENTS

DEVOTION

Both fate and family brought me to baking.

In high school I fantasized about being a chemist. I thought I'd be a scientist when I grew up. But unexpectedly, philosophy is what swept me away in my first year of university. By the end of my degree in social anthropology and development studies, I was truly confused about what career lay ahead for me. I had fallen for catering through a part-time job. I was enamoured with cultural theory. And I still longed for science. All the same, I was feeling done with theories and essays, wanting to get my hands into something, something tactile, something good.

More than my career, I was also confused about love. Feeling a need for independence upon finishing school at twenty-two, I had abruptly ended my first true love...with a German. Even though it felt like the right decision, it hurt. I coped by hosting dance parties and by indulging in my love for many things German, including a fascination with rye bread.

At the time I was living with a German named Anna Sophia and we would dabble in, and often fail at, making sourdoughs at home together. In my pursuit of hands-on learning and adventure, travel was on my mind. She eventually connected me with a farm in Germany that often hosted new people, where a friend of hers was living. The farm was adjacent to a bakery that baked for the farm and was willing to take me on. So, with very modest savings, minimal memorized vocabulary, and a one-way ticket, I took a leap of faith, all alone, into this great Germanic unknown. I could never have guessed how much I would fall for bread and bakery life, let alone how it would quickly lead to running a sourdough bakery. My scientific and philosophical inclinations could finally come together.

Everything was new during this overwhelming November overseas. I truly had no idea what my days would be like, but I soon found out I would be spending the mornings doing farm chores like shovelling hay or cleaning soil from root veggies. Since I had experience in catering, one of my farm chores that didn't involve frigid temperatures and cold hands was to cook up Canadian recipes for the shared lunch that fed the twenty of us who lived and worked on the farm.

My afternoons were always free. I would nap, study German, and go for long walks by myself along worn paths. While wandering and taking in the impressions of the countryside, I'd recall vocabulary and sometimes make my way into town for a midday German institution featured in almost every cafe and restaurant—kaffee und kuchen. Coffee and cake. After having the afternoon to myself, I'd participate in what is called abendt brotessen, a simple nightly supper ritual devoted to bread and an accompaniment of delicious spreads, cheeses, and meats. After supper, I'd meander in the dark down to the farm's bakery, Backstube Rosales, often stopping to take a deep breath and listen to the soothing swooping sound of the local windmill. Over the following six hours and with a mighty bake team of three, I'd help make fresh yeasted and sourdough breads. The evening would turn to night as we were mixing doughs, then folding, shaping, dividing, and decorating hundreds of loaves. The next morning, when I was rising for my farm chores, a few local farms—including the farm where I lived, called Örkhof—would swing by to pick up their loaves, and carry them off to sell at local markets and farm stores.

I had worked in a catering kitchen through college, but this was my first time in a bakery. Immediately romanticized by the aromas and the toasty vibes created by the never-ending but slow release of heat from stone ovens, I had found a new German love.

I was surprised to find dozens of styles of breads reflecting Germany's deep and true love of all things grain. Fluffy white bread was just one selection of a vast bread menu. We made bread from the flours of many grains, such as spelt, rye, and buckwheat. These diverse grains became breads and baked goods offering various flavours and textures. Backstube Rosales had its own flour mill. Some of the flours we used came from established organic mills, while some were grown by nearby farms and milled on-site at their respective farms. My baker's spirit was ever expanding, as I got to see how grains are grown, milled, and baked in a relatively small loop. This short chain from field, to oven, to table taught me to think about flour in new ways. I was witness to how a bakery can strengthen the local food economy while also producing delicious, healthy, and sustainable whole-grain breads. I would spend three months working at Örkhof and Backstube Rosales, learning the language and ways of the farm and bakery.

Before returning to Canada, I had the opportunity to do an unpaid apprenticeship, or praktikum, in a second bakery. This time, on an organic biodynamic farm named Dottenfelderhof, renowned among the young German farmers I was trying to befriend. It was a thousand years old, had originally been a royal farm producing for a Kaiser, and much later became an agricultural religious monastery. This latest iteration began in the 1970s, through devotees of Rudolf Steiner, a philosopher whose concepts would go on to be instrumental in the founding of biodynamic agricultural practices in Germany. Steiner had rejected the then-modern idea of using chemical fertilizers to increase yields, and argued a farm should be viewed as an entity, or an organism, unto itself, sustained by its own inputs and outputs, such as animal food and manure. By the time I arrived to do my practicum in 2008, it had morphed into a one-hundred-person biodynamic community, featuring a wood-fired bakery and an agricultural philosophy school. They also grew and milled grain on-site, creating special milling practices and textures of grain tailored to their recipes.

The bakery on Dottenfelderhof was much larger than my last, consisting of two separate baking teams for a total of twelve full-time bakers. All through the night the bread-baking crew (including yours truly) took care of breads and yeasted pastries, such as croissants. In the morning, when we bread bakers were done, the fancy cake bakers arrived. It was their job to turn out many of the sweets sold at the not-so-modest organic grocery store located on the farm.

I spent months here, giving myself over to baking, working an unpaid, six day-a-week practicum. As my hands took on the body memory, I was also seeing the integration of chemistry and philosophy that unfolded nightly within this industrious, creative bakery. The head baker was one of the few English speakers in the bakery, and he would often pull me aside to share how biodynamic principles were reflected in the process of bread making.

Whereas my bakery shifts at the farm were from 6:00 P.M. until midnight, at Dottenfelderhof, the shifts went from midnight to 8:00 A.M. After each shift, I'd take languid walks across the farm in the early spring morning back to my farm dormitory, shared with other praktikantin. I felt a sweet righteousness when I indulged in breakfast right before bed, knowing what the bakers and I had accomplished, eating silently alongside my farmmates who were just starting their workday.

By the time I left Germany six months later, I was obsessed with baking. I became fully enamoured with the beauty of the precise-yet-chaotic and efficient-yet-laborious process of working together to handcraft thousands of buns, croissants, and loaves of bread through the darkness of the night while the rest of the world around us slept.

I had sought out tactile teachings and adventure by going to Germany. What I found was a process of learning by doing and listening, an experience that became the foundation of my baking craft. Upon my return to Canada, I was still confused about my future career. But I knew I wanted to make a job for myself where I could practice the baking traditions I had just learned. Bringing these recipes to life felt obvious, given the lack of whole grain offerings in local markets. More importantly, there was something I knew I wanted to bring into my own bakery. I wanted to emulate German bakeries who relied on a spectrum of grains and flours. I wanted to show my community what else was possible. Those possibilities were made in my own wood-fired sourdough whole-grain bakery, Gold Island Bakery.

This book reflects my fifteen years of experience working with that wide spectrum of grains and flours. It will shed light on how you too can bring the joy of whole-grain baking into your life with seven unique grains and flavours: rye, oats, corn, spelt, Kamut, buckwheat, and wheat. Throughout the book, I'll be sharing some important lessons of the winding path of my baker's life, including some of my most formative encounters and baking teachers.

Both fate and family had brought me to baking. As such, this book will also reach all the way back to the influence of the women in my family who first taught me to bake while I was growing up. Within these stories, I will share some cherished family recipes and reflections on my first baking teachers, the women in my family.

The biggest baker in my heart was my grandmother Jean Anne Stevens, also known as Nan. I wouldn't be a baker without her. So much of her is laced throughout this book. In part, *Rise* is a devotion to Jean Anne. She was still making a batch of cookies here and there at age ninety-two when I first imagined this book with my editor, Simon. Soon after, she passed, and my relationship to baking and to her recipes changed. I've grieved her through this process.

Death has a way of reorienting everything, sometimes in the smallest ways. I've come to expect when I lose someone that my social orbits will be affected and my relationships will change. Energies shift, people turn onto new pathways. This reflects the natural ways that families evolve over time. They spin out differently and form new clusters of relations. Nan was in hospital, just twenty minutes from my bakery, for close to a month before dying. For a time she was bouncing back and we were planning her return home. She wanted to make it home, and she wanted pie at her homecoming. Planning on making pie for Jean was part of how I coped with coming to terms with her frailness, though her sense of humour never skipped a beat. I imagined a cacophony of pie, some homemade, some purchased, all fruity.

Some months after her death, the pandemic began. Unlike many people during lockdown, I wasn't keeping busy with baking. Instead, I went back to school to study environmental and food education while setting up a new baker, Stephen, to step into my previous role at Gold Island Bakery. This meant I could go back to school and make space for a big, beautiful cookbook project. While figuring out my research project in 2021 (yes, this cookbook is, in part, my research project), I turned back to my original dream for *Rise* and Nan's recipes. I had known all along that I wanted my grandmother's recipes to be involved. For one, they're delicious. They also shaped me and tell beautiful stories not just of the history of my family but of the history of my home.

There were a couple of things specifically left to me in Jean's will. One, her handmade quilts. Two, her cookbooks. She had moved a couple of times in her eighties and even in her nineties, so her cookbook collection was pared down but certainly not sparse. The cookbooks that remained often came from places she had travelled to, or considered close to home. She also left me a brimming wire-coiled notebook of hers. Each page contained a recipe and a credit to its author, copied out in her perfected, uncrowded, and elegant cursive. Every other page held a slip of folded paper, someone else's handwritten recipe card or a newspaper cutout. This notebook contains 333 recipes. Yes, I counted. I couldn't know if she even baked them all, but it was obvious in some cases, as she sometimes left notes for her future self, suggestions and impressions.

While reading through each recipe, I noticed quickly the diligence that Jean took in naming who had either shared it or created it. Her citation practice was impeccable. She revealed parts of herself—her wider network of local cooks, her family, and what newspapers and magazines she was reading. Through her notebook, I got to know my grandmother better, even after she was gone. The recipes inside connected me to memories of those dishes, those sweets, those holidays and moments.

Recipes written by family members stuck out to me. Many of them came from aunts and even my cousins and me—like an old vegan chocolate cake recipe I had passed on to Nan to help support her in accommodating the diet choices of my early twenties. In the time since my grandmother's passing, her family has dispersed. This most often feels like a loss to me, but baking the recipes given to Nan by my family members helps ease that. When I bake recipes from the women of my family, I assemble the ingredients like they've done so many times, I go through the same series of steps, witness the same chemical transformations they have. For an hour or two while making, and then after when tasting, I can imagine myself more easily in their shoes, their lives.

Many of the recipes in the second section of *Rise*, beginning on page 141, are adaptations of recipes from aunts and great-grandmothers. I connect to them, bringing their recipes and legacies forward into my time and family traditions, and my way of baking. Bringing together my love for experimenting with whole-grain flours and my love for family recipes is something I hope you will feel confident doing, after working through what *Rise* has to offer.

Like me, Jean thrived when feeding people, sharing a nurturing kind of love that transcended family. The final page of her abundant red notebook of recipes was a poem she had written for the menu board in the hospital where she worked, dated August of 1989. Jean's work ethic included the creations she made, available to anyone who happened to be in line for it, whether or not it was a hospital cafeteria line or a bread line at a farmers' market. The poem was

sweet and playful, a side fundamental to who my grandmother was.

Food work is practical but also creative and emotional, with room for play, especially for Jean. One of the ways I could tell whether or not Jean had tried a recipe was whether she had written down feedback or notes. As for the poem, she had written in the margins "you fool!" I leave you with her words…a recipe for summer fun, when the sun is shining for us.

Enjoy the summer while you may
Time is slipping fast away.
Shady lanes and Sunny Bowers
Ripening grain & blooming flowers.
Moonlit skies and waters blue
Sparkling Surf and Morning dew.
Summer's only what you make it—
So—guys & gals—
get out and shake it.
–Jean Stevens

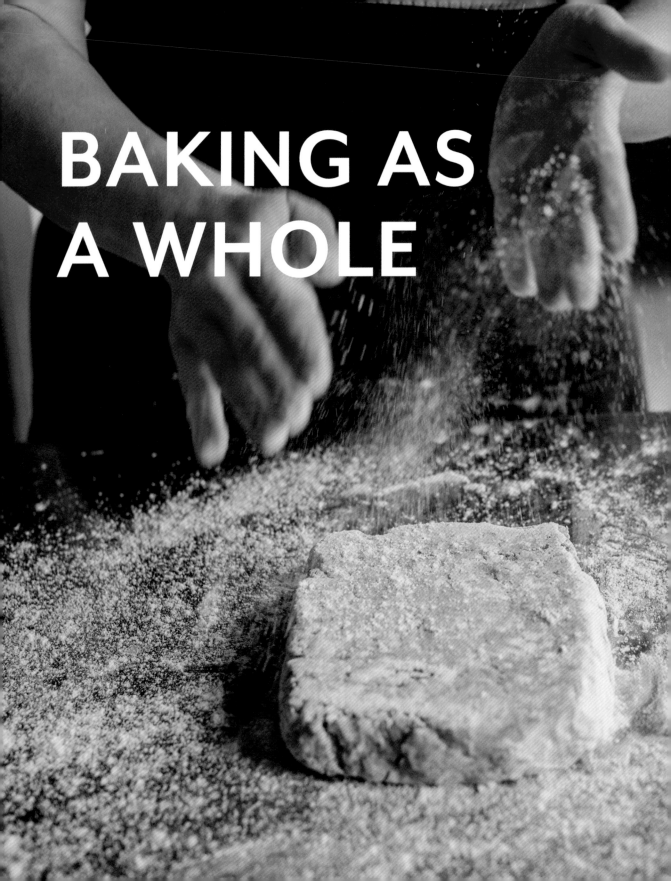

BAKING AS A WHOLE

t's important to me that everyone can learn how to bake with as few barriers as possible. Therefore, the recipes shared in this book are written so that they can be baked with minimal equipment. However, a dough scraper, a good whisk, and a rubber spatula are tools I consider essential to a basic baking set-up. Most recipes can be made in a variety of baking vessels and with little else than a few medium-sized bowls and measuring tools.

Baking with whole grains is not as different or as difficult as you may think. Whole grains and whole-grain baked goods have become increasingly accessible, affordable, and delicious thanks to dedicated farmers, millers, and bakers around the world reclaiming and redefining what it means to bake. Countless teachers have been an inspiration to me and my baking practice. Without them, I wouldn't be where I am, or here with you at home.

The first thing to do is to source your whole-grain flours. This, too, is much easier than you may think. Check out bulk-food stores, or spots where organic food is sold. (Also, see Grain Sources, beginning on page 177.) Farmers' markets are great because you may even be able to get that grain straight from the source. More and more national grocery chains are selling whole-grain flours on their shelves, including flours that may come from your own province, or one nearby. If you live in an area that sells organic, local, or fairly traded foods, such as an independently owned grocer or co-op, you should be able to find a great selection of flours and grains, some even grown near you.

The "whole" in whole grain reminds us that grains are perishable. This is unfortunate, as the real flavour of whole-grain baked foods, as well as the nutrition, comes from the perishable parts of grains, namely the bran and the germ. The bran and germ lose their nutritional value as time goes on due to oxidation, which can lead to "off" flavours. This may be another reason why some people believe they don't like whole-grain baked goods, as most of what you've probably had has been made with whole grain flours that weren't stored properly.

All-purpose flours have all of the bran or germ removed from them, meaning there is no nutritional loss as it sits on a shelf. It also doesn't really have a flavour unto itself, as the bran carries a lot of the taste of grain, as well as the nutrients! Most of the time, millers will place a "best by" date that is on or near the milling or packing date of the flour. When buying, look at the expiration date on your flour; since whole-grain flours have a shorter shelf life, find one with the closest date to your purchase.

The kind of grains, and their respective flours, you use will also affect the textures and appearance of the dough. For example, the texture of baked goods made with whole rye flour are different than those made with a light (sifted) rye or a wheat flour. But that variation is the beauty here. You can make your baking your own.

The recipes and tips shared in *Rise* can equip any home baker with the methods to explore the realm of possibilities that whole-grain flours open up in your baking.

BAKING
BASICS & TIPS

Sharing my knowledge of whole grains is one of my favourite aspects of teaching people how to bake. I believe strongly in meeting people where they are, whether that is in terms of how well acquainted they are with baking, or how well stocked their kitchen is. When I teach classes on whole-grain baking, I don't just give out recipes. I often give out all kinds of tips, pointing out things I've learned and been taught over the years.

People often think that baking requires doing things *just so,* so when I teach, I'm not interested in being precious about it. Many of the recipes in this book have tips and tricks that will help strengthen your baking skills in general, while also making a whole-grain baker out of you! To get you started, check out these pointers which will help you work through many of the recipes in this book.

ESSENTIAL TOOLS

You don't need much to bake bread! A heavy bread pan, a good-sized (medium-large) bowl, a digital scale, and a dough scraper (a flexible plastic one is better than a rigid metal one, though I like having both in my set-up).

HAND MIXING VS. MACHINE

Use your hands. I love involving my hands in baking. They have the capacity to manipulate ingredients like no other, and there is no better way to learn what various doughs feel like at various stages. I really recommend using your hands for *mixing bread doughs* so you can feel the texture and learn a lot about your dough this way, *folding egg whites into a cake batter,* to integrate them as quickly and delicately as possible, as well as *folding in flour,* especially while trying not to overmix.

Having said that, I own both an inherited stand mixer and hand mixer for baking. While I do love the stand mixer for buttercream and for dough mixing while busy, I wouldn't prioritize it over having easy-to-store electric whisks/beaters on hand. Owning a solid whisk, thick with strong tines, is essential regardless of whether you have an electric mixer. A good whisk can, with elbow grease, work just as well as an electric tool.

box grater

dry measuring cups

pastry blender

silicon spatula

sieve

liquid measuring cup

measuring spoons

thermometer

rasp/zester

rolling pin

hand mixer

plastic dough scraper

pastry brush

scale

measuring tape

potato masher

whisk

offset spatula

FOLDING DOUGH

As bakers, we can further the development of the gluten in our doughs by kneading and folding the doughs. In grains like wheat, spelt, and Kamut, the gluten is being continuously developed into alignment, by virtue of the carbon dioxide released through fermentation, slowly expanding the dough, passively stretching the gluten. Wetter or higher hydration doughs can be harder to manipulate by hand, especially whole-grain doughs. The following is a folding technique that I consider a gentle kneading technique.

• When you return to your sticky dough during the bulk fermentation, heavily dust a work surface with flour (all-purpose or a whole-grain flour sifted with a fine sieve).

• Using a flexible dough scraper, turn your fermented (likely slack) dough ball onto the floured surface. With floured hands, attempt to only touch the parts of the dough that have become floured when transfering from the bowl onto your bench. Your dough ball will likely flatten out. If not, you can take floured fingers, spread apart, and press them quickly into the dough, spreading it out in one press.

• Take the points of the dough circle at 9 and 3 o'clock, stretch them gently by pulling the dough away from the centre, then fold them together into the centre. Repeat this with 12 and 6 o'clock. You can repeat this whole process once or twice if getting maximum volume is the goal with your loaf.

TRYING TO MIMIC A BAKERY AT HOME

Make sure the room and ingredients aren't cold. This is especially important for the bulk fermentation period of the dough. If the dough is cool when you finish the initial mixing and kneading phase *and* the room temperature is cool, your sourdough loaf may be doomed.

Make a proofer at home: your kitchen might not be a bakery, but you can insert a pan of boiling water into a lightly preheated (and then turned off) oven to make a proofing chamber.

BUTTER

Temperature

If a recipe states a preference for the temperature of the butter, follow the directions. The temperature of butters impact how they are integrated into the baked good, as well as how they behave when baking.

What's the difference between room-temperature vs. softened butter? If you are mixing recipe batters electrically, it doesn't matter as much if your room temperature butter is on the softer or harder side. If mixing by hand, however, sometimes you must soften the butter, either in the microwave for a few seconds or by preheating an oven briefly on low and tempering the butter on an ovenproof plate or bowl.

Salt or Unsalted?

I recommend for most recipes to just use whatever butter you have on hand, but know that there is about ¼ tsp of salt per ½ cup of butter in salted butter. With little exception, the recipes in this book were made using salted butter. If you are watching your salt content, by all means use unsalted butter.

For certain recipes like cookies and cakes, you can get away with swapping butter for vegetable shortening, solid coconut oil, or margarine. Any recipe that asks for a liquid fat is usually good with these substitutions. For the purposes of pastry, like pie, cold shortening (vegetable- or animal-based) works well, as do vegan butter baking sticks. Margarine or coconut oil are not recommended for pie.

EGGS

Using room-temperature eggs can make your baking experience a little easier. They integrate a little more easily into batters, and when whisking, they will integrate air a lot faster than when cold, especially if you are whipping egg whites by hand. If your eggs are cold and you need to warm them up quickly, place them in a bowl filled with very hot water for a couple of minutes.

To separate an egg, I either crack it and then strain the white through my fingers (use those hands!) or carefully crack an egg in half, keeping its contents in the larger half of the cracked egg shell. Next I carefully tip the shell around so the white pours out and the yolk stays behind.

Note that using extra-large eggs or small eggs can throw off the moisture content of your recipes. This isn't always significant but it is worth noting. Market eggs tend to be larger than standard grocery store large eggs.

MILK

In most recipes, especially those that don't involve the heating or cooking of milk, swapping soy, oat, or other non-dairy milks totally works. Do keep in mind, however, that many non-dairy milks have added sugar and other flavourings such as vanilla, so adjust your recipe accordingly.

SUGAR

I use organic cane sugar as an all-purpose sugar in my kitchen and bakery. It performs quite close to white sugar, and the recipes in this book are made to be used by home bakers using either. The only exception are meringues, which may have a different texture due to the cane sugar. I still use it for this recipe, but if you are trying to replicate a classic, stick to white sugar.

Coarseness of sugar varies, so if experimenting with non-white sugars, look for finer sugars, especially when you need to cream sugar and butter. Conventional brown sugar is white sugar with some molasses added back in. This means if you have white (or cane) sugar at home, you can add 1 tsp of molasses to offer the same flavouring as brown sugar.

YOUR OVEN

Your oven at home is not like my oven, or your neighbour's oven. They all have their quirks, and the most common one is temperature. Invest in an oven thermometer to see what temperature your oven is *actually* performing at. Chances are it may be anywhere from fifteen to thirty degrees off, and that can and will affect your baking.

Investing in a pizza stone or baker's stone is an inexpensive way to regulate the temperature of your home oven. Pizza stones have more thermal mass than baking pans, holding on to heat and tempering or evening out the heat from electric oven elements. They are also great for free-form baking. (See: "baking stone" in the Glossary on page 19 for more.)

COMMON SUBSTITUTIONS

Substitution is not a dirty word. It's a way for you to play with baking and see what works best for you. Here are some of the substitutions I find work best in the recipes in this book.

Spices

If you are missing a spice for a recipe, you may have one of its cousins nearby. If you are wondering if one spice might be replaced by another, use your nose to see if it's complimentary to the spice mix. For example: cardamom for nutmeg, or ginger for cinnamon.

Vanilla or baking alcohols

Out of vanilla but have an old bottle of spiced rum or Amaretto around? Use it in your baking instead. Don't feel like picking up brandy for the sprouted grain mincemeat? Experiment with some liqueurs you do have on hand. Cointreau and other orange-based liqueurs are great in baking.

Whole wheat, whole spelt, and whole Kamut flours

These will often work as substitutions for each other in many of the *Rise* recipes. Similarly, many gluten-free whole-grain flours can be substituted for each other. Just know whatever the dominant properties of your chosen grain are, be they flavour or texture, you are introducing them into your recipe.

GREASING PANS

Save your butter wrappers. After you've used your butter, the foil wrapper is perfect for greasing a pan. Other options include pouring a small drizzle of oil in the pan and then coating the inside surface of the pan with it, using a pastry brush or small square of paper towel.

For cakes, the extra step of flouring your greased pan will help lift the cake from the pan once baked. To do this, add a teaspoon of a sifted, finely milled or all-purpose flour to your greased pan and then tilt the pan around until the flour has been evenly distributed and coated the inside.

COOLING ON A RACK VS. THE PAN

I go back and forth between using a cooling rack and not using one when baking for myself. However, cakes that require flipping out of a pan rely on cooling racks the most. When a cake is trapped in a pan, the pan can get soggy. In a pinch, you can carefully transfer a cake to a plate after it cools in the pan for at least 15 minutes.

TIME

Baking takes time, but the best baking uses time to its advantage. Whole-grain flours behave differently when given time, not only in terms of proofing doughs (see Essentials of Bread Baking, page 25) or remembering to feed your starter the night before, but also in the finished texture of certain baked goods. Cookie doughs and brownie batters benefit greatly from being left to their own devices in the fridge for a few hours, or even overnight. The difference between a just-mixed and baked dough/batter versus one that has been given ample time to bloom and develop will change the way you bake.

WEIGHT OR VOLUME?

Something to know about whole-grain flours is various grains will have various weights. Unlike all-purpose flour, which weighs the same every time, one cup of stone-ground spelt flour will likely vary in weight from another whole ground spelt flour. This also means that 125 g of one rye flour may equal 1 cup but 125 g of a different rye flour may be actually pretty far off.

This is all to say that *measuring the weight of your flour provides you with a constant that cup measurements don't.* Always weighing your ingredients, you can observe how 200 g of one whole-grain flour behaves, compared to the same amount of a differently milled flour.

LEVEL, SCANT, AND HEAPING

For best results with baking in general, use a scale. But even if you don't have access to one, a good tip is to fill your cup or measuring device using a spoon or another item. Avoid dipping your cup directly into your flour, as it can lead to imprecise measurements. Here are some terms to keep in mind if measuring without a scale.

Level

When I want to be precise, I gently drag the flat side of a butter knife over the full cup measure (over a bowl so I don't waste the flour).

Scant

When you shake the measuring cup to level the contents, and it's just a little less than full.

Heaping

When the measure cup is just a little bit over full.

METRIC VS. US CUSTOMARY

All throughout this book you will see recipes using both metric and US customary (formerly known as Imperial measurements).

In *Rise,* we use US customary cups, in which there are 237 milliliters. 1 US cup is also equivalent to just under 16 tablespoons. So often when I am scaling recipes and using cups instead of weights, I will work out the modifications using tablespoon increments. One metric cup is 250 ml but is rarely used as the millilitre amount is referred to instead.

When it comes to small amounts, such as teaspoons, I often only write in the amount using the teaspoon, as scales for such small amounts aren't necessary. This usually applies to things like spices, or chemical leavens like baking soda or baking powder.

SIFTING AND WHISKING DRY INGREDIENTS

Sifting your flour using a mesh sieve ensures that every clump is busted and the flour has the maximum amount of aeration, which makes the blending of dry and wet ingredients smoother. If you have any bran left over in your sieve, just add it back in to your dry ingredients.

Whisks work great for this too, especially when you don't notice much clumping in your dry mix.

FLOUR FOR DUSTING

When rolling cookie doughs or kneading bread, flour is often dusted over a smooth surface to ensure it doesn't stick. When baking breads, I dust with the flour I am using for said bread (rye for rye breads, etc.). In the case of more delicate doughs, such as pie pastry, I often use all-purpose flour, as it is fine enough not to impact the final product. (See: "dusting flour" in the Glossary, page 20.)

FRESH FLOUR VS. STALE FLOUR

We aren't used to thinking about flour in terms of freshness or aliveness. Whole-grain flours are living foods with oily and enzymatically active parts, and those parts don't age well! As a rule of thumb, try and buy no more than 6 months worth of whole grain flour at a time, less in the summer, longer in the winter. You can freeze flour in an airtight container if you pick up a speciality flour you want to last.

All-purpose white flour has a long shelf life due to it being stripped of the elements that aren't shelf stable, while the shelf life of a whole-grain flour can vary, depending on when it was milled and how it was stored. The flour you just bought at your local grocer or bulk store may be new to you, but it may have been sitting for a while, as many of these vendors want products that can last on their shelves for up to a year. Watch for signs of flour moths at bulk food shops.

To remedy this, many producers can be contacted directly to find out milling dates based on various product codes, or even best-before dates on your flour. Chances are, the best-before date is one year to the day that the flour was milled.

STEEL- VS. STONE-MILLED FLOURS

Most if not all stone-ground flours will state on their packaging how their flour was milled. 99.9% of white flour is made in a steel mill, so when in doubt, assume it is steel-milled. Steel-milled flours tend to be a lot finer and silkier in texture than stone-ground flours, and steel-milled whole-grain flours are great for when you want your whole-grain baking to most closely resemble white flour baking results.

Steel mills get extremely hot and tend to pasteurize flours as they are milled, whereas stone-milled flours stay cooler and often retain some living features like yeasts and enzymes. Most small-scale or artisan flour mills use stone mills, which are highly adjustable. This means that all stone-ground flours are unique, and coarseness and texture will vary widely even among flours made from the same grain. Stone-ground flours have coarser and bigger pieces of bran, and as such, absorb water more slowly. This makes them ideal for bread making, where your dough takes hours to mature.

GLOSSARY

I n keeping with recipes that anyone can use, I am also aware that in using whole-grain flours (not to mention sourdough starters) there is often a need for a little extra information. The vocabulary used in baking (and baking books) can sometimes seem a little opaque to the occasional or beginner baker. That's unfortunate, because baking is about clarity: of process, of needs, of observation. *This* ingredient yields *this* result via *this* process.

Here you will find words that I use in this book, as well as tips on various ingredients, techniques, and more. Some of these are words I purposefully don't use in the recipes to ensure the clarity I am after, but I think it's still helpful to demystify the language of baking. If you're a big word geek like me, you're going to come across these words in other baking books, and amongst other bakers. For a list of some of those books, see the Bibliography on page 180.

ACIDS, ACETIC AND LACTIC: Along with carbon dioxide, acetic and lactic acids are the by-products of fermentation, which help give flavour to various fermented foods. Acetic acid is more citrusy and bright, while lactic is tangy and tart. The ratio of each in your sourdough starter will impact the final bake. According to some bakers, a thinner starter left in warmer temperatures produces more lactic acid, while a thicker starter in a colder temperature favours more acetic.

BAKING STONE: A somewhat generic term for any kind of block of unglazed tile or stone placed in an oven. Baking stones can serve to regulate the temperature of a home oven, as it traps and keeps heat. They can also be used to bake breads directly on top of. If using one in your oven, allow the oven to stay at the designated preheating temperature for at least 15 minutes (or longer) to ensure an even temperature. Baking stones tend to be sold as squares or rectangles, while pizza stones are round, yet serve the same purpose.

BAKING POWDER: Composed of two parts, usually baking soda (an alkaline/base) and an acid (such as cream of tartar), which, when combined with liquid, gives off carbon dioxide gas. Baking powder also often reacts not only to this initial mixing but also to heat from the oven, giving both an initial lift as well as a subsequently during the baking process.

BAKING SODA OR BICARBONATE OF SODA: An alkaline powder that, when combined with an acid, produces carbon dioxide, providing a rise in baked goods. Baked goods made with only baking soda should be baked as quickly as possible after mixing, as the gas is released relatively quickly.

BARLEY: *Hordeum vulgare,* or barley, is used in baking, brewing, and as a food unto itself across countries and cultures. When used as a flour, barley brings a caramel-like sweetness, especially when the flour is toasted before mixing into doughs. Barley flour is great in cookies, especially in the bottom layer of squares where the natural sugars present in the flour can bring out a toffee-like sweetness. Malted barley flour (See: "malting") is often used in commercial baking products, such as certain crackers, to give more dimension of flavour. Think of the distinct flavour found in Ovaltine or digestive biscuits. Worth seeking out.

BRAN: The hard outer layer of cereal grains, oil and high in fibre. Bran is perishable, meaning that it usually has a shelf life of anywhere from 3–6 months, depending on how it is stored.

CORN, CORNMEAL, CORN FLOUR: Corn can be milled (and sifted) to varying degrees. For the purposes of this book, cornmeal and corn flour are used. Remember that corn, like all grains, is most flavourful when recently milled. Check the health food section of your local grocer for locally milled cornmeal. Finely milled corn flour is soft textured and great for cookies and cakes. Naturally free of gluten, it is often used as a textural contrast and flavour booster in various baked goods. *Note:* Corn flour is the term used in the UK to describe what North Americans call cornstarch. In this book, corn flour refers to the silky-textured flour used in the Orange Blossom Corn Cake on page 74.

CRUMB: This is the term used to refer to the interior structure of a loaf. That structure is the result of carbon dioxide being trapped by the gluten (or other proteins) developed during baking. The holes you see are where the gas reaction of the yeast once stretched and aligned the gluten into strands around the bubbles emerging in the dough. *Open crumb* refers to an open structure, indicating that the loaf was well

fermented. When dough is under-fermented, the yeasts and/or gluten structure are not strong enough to support an open structure. When over-fermented, the dough or gluten strength can break down, no longer able to support the structure of the loaf.

DEGAS, DEGASSING: Sometimes called *punching* or *punching down*, it is the act of releasing the gasses trapped in a dough, to help in the proofing process.

DOUGH SCRAPER: A metal or plastic square, often with a rounded handle, used to shape and cut dough as well as scrape dough off of counters or places where the dough has been kneaded.

DUSTING FLOUR: A neutral flour used for dusting over your kneading area. With whole-grain baking, this can be done with all-purpose flour if you like, but any well-milled and fine whole-grain flour can work here, preferably a flour that has a lower protein content (known as "soft wheat") is best here.

ENDOSPERM: The inner part of grains, high in starch, and where the proteins that form gluten are contained. This component of the grain is also where most of the energy is stored.

ENZYMES: The chemicals that help break starches down into simpler sugars. Enzymes are essential in plant germination as they help make the sugars in seeds (and therefore grains) accessible for the sprout to emerge and root in the earth. Every seed (and therefore every grain) has all the energy it needs to grow a sprout which becomes the root of a plant, then capable of drawing up energy from the soil instead of the energy reserve in the seed. See, bread is a superfood made of seed energy! The enzymes are contained in the germ, a component of whole-grain flours that is removed to make white flour. When we bake with whole-grain flours, we are working with the enzymes and they become a part of the chemistry of our sourdough fermentations, different from a white sourdough. Rye is very enzymatically active, which is one of the reasons it makes for such vigorous sourdough.

ENRICHED DOUGH: A dough that contains either eggs, sugar, fat, or dairy (usually milk). Brioche and challah are examples of enriched doughs.

FATS: Different fats behave in different ways. Keep in mind that they all have different melting points.

FLAKES/ROLLED FLAKES: Grains that have been cooked or roasted, steamed, and then rolled into flakes. Commonly flaked grains include oats and rye.

GERM: The part of cereal grains from which the plant germinates. High in fats and vitamins, and highly perishable. Wheat germ is the most common form available for baking.

GLUTEN: A combination of proteins created when water and flour mix, gluten is what helps bread and other baked goods keep their shape. It is comprised mainly of two proteins, glutenin (which provides strength and helps the dough spring back once stretched) and gliadin (which helps it extend without breaking or going slack). Flours that are high in these proteins and therefore develop stronger gluten are more often used in making breads, while lower-protein flours are used in pastry and cake making. (See: "wheat, soft" and "wheat, hard".)

HYDRATION: The amount of water, usually presented as a percentage, that is included in a particular bread. The calculation of that percentage is often called Baker's Math. For example, If you have a dough made with 100 grams of flour and 90 grams of water, you have a bread with 90% hydration.

KAMUT/KHORASAN WHEAT: Technically two terms used for the same grain. Kamut is the trademarked name for Khorasan, a variety of wheat named for a region which now encapsulates parts of Northen Iran and Afghanistan. In the US, the trademarked name "Kamut" is used when the grain is grown with specific seeds and under specific growing requirements, such as in an organic manner. (See pages 100–101 for details.)

MALTING, MALTED: Flour milled from grains that have been soaked and sprouted, starting an enzymatic activity within the grain which changes the flavour. Malting also brings out natural sweetness in grains, but with a much more complex flavour profile. (See: Malted Grains on page 52.)

MILLING: the act of rendering grains and pseudocereals into viable flour(s). The act of milling impacts various aspects of the flour, from shelf-life to baking qualities.

NUTS: Nuts, like grains, are perishable foodstuffs, and should be treated as such. The fat in nuts is what makes them so delicious, but it can and does oxidize over time, turning rancid. It's always good to purchase them from stores and suppliers that have high turnover rates, such as bulk- or international food stores like Middle Eastern grocers. If you aren't able to do so, place nuts in the fridge or freezer until needed. Walnuts tend to be the biggest culprit when it comes to rancidity, followed by hazelnuts, then almonds.

OVEN SPRING: Oven spring refers to when the dough first enters the oven and there is a frenzy of yeast activity (whether dry active or sourdough), giving off gases that contribute to the rise in the dough.

The final proofing of dough is a key step in creating good oven spring, ensuring that when the dough enters the oven, the yeasts are active enough to explode and give the biggest rise of all to open the crumb of your loaf, as well as the development and strength of the gluten in the bread. If the final proof goes too long, your loaf may come out with a flat top, all of the bread dough having sunk to the bottom. This is called a *flying roof* or a *flying crust*. There must be enough energy for this final fermentation frenzy, and if the dough is spent, then you will not get a spring. (To support this, see tips on proofing and scoring in Baking Basics.)

PRE-FERMENTS: A pre-ferment is small amount of dough or sponge that is used to bring flavour to baked goods, often leavened with commercial or instant yeasts. It is usually made the night before baking. There are various types of pre-ferments, with the most typical names/variations being the *poolish* (a wet dough, almost batter-like in consistency, often made of equal parts water and flour) and the *biga* (made with less water than flour, for a stiffer pre-ferment).

PSEUDOCEREALS: Foods that are used, eaten, or milled in the same manner as cereal grains but are not botanically part of the cereal family. Examples of pseudocereals include buckwheat, amaranth, and quinoa.

SALT: Salt helps deliver flavour to baked goods and helps retard the proofing process by changing the pH of the dough. When I bake I use fine salt, usually sea salt because it is less processed than table salt and contains natural minerals. I find 1 teaspoon of fine sea salt generally equals 7 grams.

SCALD(ING): Flours are scalded by pouring boiling water over them. This gelatinizes the proteins in the flour, helping to raise the amount of liquid or water in the dough, which can also help improve the shelf life of baked goods. Doughs made from non-wheat and lower-gluten flours such as rye or buckwheat are often scalded.

SOAKERS: A small amount of seeds, kernels, bran, or flour that has been soaked for a period of time to soften it. By pre-soaking these items, you prevent them from absorbing too much liquid from your final dough, helping the shelf life and texture of the final product.

SPONGE: See: pre-ferments.

SUGAR(S): All of the recipes in this book were made using *granulated sugar* or a fine evaporated cane sugar unless noted in the recipe. Granulated sugar is made from refining sugarcane or sugar beets. Part of that refining process yields molasses.

Brown sugar is white sugar that has had molasses re-introduced into it. The degree of molasses determines whether your brown sugar is light or dark. Brown sugars will yield more caramel or toffee flavours to your baked goods. If you ever run out of brown sugar, simply add a small amount of molasses to your white granulated sugar.

Demerara sugar is granulated sugar that has not had the molasses extracted from it. *Icing* or *confectioner's sugar* is finely ground sugar with cornstarch added to prevent clumping.

Beyond acting as a sweetener and flavouring, sugars also help determine the final texture and shelf life of baked goods. The moisture content of the sugar as well as the size of the grains of the sugar will also affect this.

WHEAT, HARD: Wheats that are high in protein, mostly used for making breads due to their gluten-forming properties. These wheats, sometimes called *winter wheats*, are planted in the fall and overwinter in the ground, having an extended growing season.

WHEAT, SOFT: Wheats that are low in protein, often used in making cakes or pastries. These wheats, sometimes called *spring wheats*, are planted in the spring and have a shorter growing season, and therefore have a lower protein content than hard wheats.

WHEAT, VARIETIES: Beyond hard and soft wheats, certain wheats are also known as spring or winter wheats, characterized by when they are sown or planted, factors which can also affect characteristics of the final flour. There are also various colours of wheats, with white and red being the most common, and refer to the general colour of the grain's husk.

There are also varietals of wheats bred for particular climates, cultures and communities, and needs. Red Fife is well known amongst Canadian bakers for making bread, while Acadia

Wheat can be found in the Maritime provinces and has been grown since the middle of the twentieth century. Other varieties include einkorn (one of the oldest varieties of wheat still cultivated by man), spelt (sometimes called an ancient grain), emmer (sometimes known as farro) which is related to durum (a high-protein wheat used in making pasta). Farmers are growing more varieties of wheat to satisfy both consumer interest and to help preserve biodiversity in wheat, as well as adapting to climate change.

WHOLE-GRAIN FLOURS: Cereals (and some pseudocereals, like buckwheat) that have been milled into flour and the grain or cereal has been left whole, so that the flour contains all of the parts of the grain, including the bran, germ, and endosperm.

WHOLE WHEAT FLOUR: Unlike whole-grain flours, most commercially available whole wheat flours are a blend of all-purpose flour with proprietary amounts of bran reintroduced and blended into it.

YEAST: Most books, including this one, ask for active dry yeast as an ingredient. This is to differentiate it from the wild yeasts that populate and form the basis of sourdough starters. Temperatures above 46°C (115°F) will kill yeast.

ESSENTIALS OF BREAD BAKING

Good bread is worthy of respect and devotion, from the first mix to the last bite. That doesn't mean making bread has to be intimidating, but I get that it can be. Most of the recipes in this book follow similar processes in mixing, rising, and baking, but beginner bakers sometimes want to know a little more than just what is in the recipe. And so before we get our hands dirty (remember, hands are your best mixers), I thought it would be good to transmit some helpful information and insights about what happens when flour and water combine.

HOW'S YOUR STARTER?

Every good sourdough loaf starts with a strong starter. What I mean by *strong* is that it hasn't fully spent the energy from the last time you fed it. This can be tough to assess at first, but there are some visual cues to look for: there are still air bubbles in your starter culture; it doesn't smell too alcoholic or acidic; and a liquid hasn't formed on top of your culture.

Ripe rye sponge.

By feeding your starter culture with a few spoonfuls of flour and water prior to making bread with it, you are initiating and building the culture up to being able to reproduce as actively as possible in your final dough, resulting in an efficiently and well risen whole-grain sourdough loaf.

1-STAGE VS. 2-STAGE DOUGH

This terminology generally distinguishes a yeasted dough (1-stage, or direct dough) from a sourdough (2-stage). With a 1-stage dough, you essentially mix all the ingredients all at once. Sourdoughs are 2-stage doughs, which means that they always have a sponge (small portion of the total flour that gets mixed with the starter culture and water and then is left to ripen) and a final dough (the ripe sponge plus more flour, water, and salt).

Exception: There are certain yeasted breads that are 2-stage doughs which use pre-ferments, often known as a *poolish* or a *biga*, where you start with a smaller-than-usual amount of dry yeast (often a ¼ tsp or so) and mix it with a small portion of the flour and water and let that sit overnight. This style mimics the sourdough process and leads to a more nuanced yeasted flavour in the finished loaf.

THE TRIANGLE OF TIME, TEMPERATURE, AND HYDRATION

Fermentations—be they dough, kraut, or other delicious foodstuffs—are determined by three overarching conditions of the ferment: time, temperature, and hydration. They all exist in close relation to each other, and changing one condition will alter the others. Waiting longer, dropping the temperature of water or adding more will alter the chemistry, timing, and results of your food. Knowing this is empowering. Over time, you can gain the skills of manipulating the conditions of the triangle to get certain textural results or to speed up the ripening of your doughs.

TEMPERATURES

Dough

A good rule of thumb is to aim for a dough temperature around 24°C / 75°F. If you have a digital thermometer (good for testing final internal temperature), you can probe your dough to see if it's within range. This temperature is ideal for the proliferation of yeasts inside the dough, meaning that your dough will ripen expediently.

Rye doughs are an exception to this rule. They can be closer to 28°C or even as high as 30°C. This shortens the fermentation time, which is advantageous for rye breads as they have higher enzyme activity. Enzymes are beneficial to sourdough fermentation but if left to their own devices for too long, they can also break down the dough and ruin the crumb or the final rise.

Water

You can most easily control the temperature of your dough with water. This is true whether or not you are measuring either the dough temperature or the water. If you want to get scientific about it, there are formulas online to help you figure out what water temperature is needed to create an ideal dough, taking into account air temperature, ingredient temperature, etc.

HYDRATION

Understanding hydration can help whole-grain bread bakers figure out how to get more volume out of their loaves. Some bakers express hydration as a percentage of how much water is in the dough. (See: "hydration" in the Glossary on page 21 for more on "Baker's Math.") In general with whole-grain bread baking, pushing how much water the dough can handle while still being workable (even if it's just barely handleable) yields great results.

A lot of whole-grain sourdough recipes (including the ones in *Rise*) create a dough that cannot be kneaded as easily as white flour doughs. The goal is to create a loaf that can be shaped into a round ball that does hold its shape (more or less) for a minute. As the dough ripens it loses structure and often becomes easier to handle, though a floured work surface and regularly flouring your hands will always be a must.

AUTOLYSE

This is a step introduced into some bread recipes that allows the water to more fully absorb into the flour by letting just-mixed flour and water sit undisturbed for a period of time, usually about 30 minutes or so. It also assists in yeast (sourdough or dry-active) reproduction getting underway. Partly, we do this as whole-grain flours absorb water slowly, and an autolyse causes the particles in the flour to swell and absorb the liquid before kneading, allowing for stronger gluten formation, and can make your initial kneading easier. Salt is always added after the autolyse phase.

BULK FERMENTATION

This is the part of the bread process where the yeasts are doing their thing, consuming all the sugars available to them in the flour and releasing gas while doing it. By kneading dough intensively to start, and then periodically during the bulk fermentation period, we are developing the gluten strands in our doughs. The very action of the gas expanding itself stretches and aligns the gluten strands, which can require a little more help as the bran in the flour can shorten or shred these strands. Both bulk fermentation and the autolyse help in gluten formation, leading to better loaves. And better yet, it's hands off: time is doing the work for us!

PROOFING

Generally speaking, proofing is the process in which the bread dough ferments and rises. Because we often talk about bulk fermentation, another use of the term *proofing* is to describe the final rise of the bread in the pan or rising in a form. This is a crucial phase of bread making because the yeasts are reproducing and creating gas that will form the eventual pore structure of your loaf. If you bake too early, the dough won't be ripe enough and won't gain the maximum rise it can. Done too late, your loaf may collapse or be extra sour. I think of it like surfing: you have to catch the wave at the right moment in its rising. Similarly, you want to catch your loaf when it is clearly active and expanding, but not yet too far. Recognizing the readiness of your proofing dough comes from the practice of making bread. Two solid rules of thumb: Whole-grain doughs should be expanded by at least 30% (Thanks, Doug!) and a dough is well proofed when you poke it firmly and the dough expands back in 5–15 seconds (Thanks, Richard!).

Proofing can also be used in reference to yeasts. Such as when testing or proofing to see if the yeasts are active. Think of the first stage of a yeasted dough where you mix the yeast, water, and often a bit of sugar to test its viability. If it bubbles up, you know your loaf can rise. If after 10 minutes there is no activity, that yeast is dead and cannot be used.

STEAM

Steam is essential to creating some of your favourite artisanal loaves. Modern professional bread ovens have advanced steam-injecting features. During the first 10–15 minutes of baking, gaseous moisture (steam) helps to caramelize the sugars in the grain of the crust of the bread while protecting/stalling the formation of the crust. This caramelization leads to some of the deeper hues of reds and mahogany possible with crust colour. Steam also really helps with what is called *oven spring*, which is the tendency of a loaf to rise quickly when it first enters the oven, as the yeasts die off and the temperature rises.

THE STARTER

Even before I left for Germany, I had set my sights on working in a German bakery to learn more about rye. I had grown up seeing imported and vacuum-sealed pumpernickel loaves in the international foods section of my local grocery store. These breads seemed to defy the definition of the bread I grew up with. They were dense, coarsely textured, and molasses-sweet, yet usually contained only rye and salt as ingredients. How could this be? What was so special about rye? What processes could yield such breads? I wanted to know more.

When I first landed in Germany in the early winter of 2008, I began to question whether flying across the Atlantic to learn more about baking had been the right decision. I struggled with living on a small farm in northwest Germany with twenty people I'd never met before. Few people spoke English and my modest traveller's vocabulary was pretty much useless for fully immersed farm living. Each morning, I had to work up the courage to head down to the large farm breakfast table.

But at breakfast, there would be bread, a reminder of why I came to Windrather Tal. There I would find brotessen, a morning and night meal featuring different breads and spreads, each place setting having its own little cutting board. As I selected the fixings for my personal breadboard, I'd take in the near-musical wall of sound produced by fifteen Germans chatting over breakfast. I'd listen for recognizable sounds or words. As I settled in, I learned to communicate and connect with people in non-verbal ways, ways that became fundamental to the informal

baking apprenticeship I would embark on. It's also where I first learned to communicate with grains.

Backstube Rosales, the organic bakery that was part-owned by the farm where I lived, was a toasty and aromatic workspace. Just like at the meal table, communication took many forms at the bakery. Run by a boisterous head baker named Enrique, who spoke German, Spanish, and English, the bakery usually felt like a relief. It was comforting to arrive at the bakery and talk with someone. But it was especially exciting to talk to Enrique about the topic of sourdough, one of my reasons for travelling to Germany. Normally, Enrique worked only with one other baker, Sina. The three of us worked well together, even if Sina and I could not speak. We figured out ways to share and communicate through body language, our own code of glances, working side by side, dividing and shaping doughs at the baker's bench. I think I was a welcome presence in the space, lightening the load as an aspiring bread nerd.

At the bakery, we mostly stuck to baking breads, about eighteen different kinds. We worked with free-form and pan loaves, with sourdough and yeasted breads. But it wasn't just the shapes of the bread that interested me. We also worked with grains grown by five different farms in the same valley as us, as well as some imported flours. Part of Enrique's daily baking prep was to freshly mill the oats, rye, and a couple other specialty grains and flours. These were milled into varying degrees of fineness or coarseness, specific to the individual styles of bread.

Every once in a while, Enrique would invite me on my afternoons off to watch him mill. Upon entering the dusty milling room, a soft aroma filled the air. While the mills were running, I'd get close to the buckets of freshly milled grain. Taking a light whiff, there was a sweet earthiness to these flours, especially the rye, giving off hints of its unique musty fragrance. Clumping some of the flour in my hand, I could feel the residual warmth produced by the stones in grinding the flour. I could get a tactile sense of the different textures Enrique was milling from these local grain, both seeing and feeling the particulates in the flours. Uniformity was not always the most important criteria here: it was about understanding what the grain could give to the miller or baker, and what the baker or miller could yield from it.

I would also occasionally tag along with Enrique to visit some of the other farms in the valley that pooled their grain harvests to be milled at Backstube Rosales. These local kernels came into our bakery as dried seeds—which is what grain kernels are—and left as transformed, fermented loaves. The hilly, lush farmscapes of this valley were a part of the flavour of our breads. The loaves reflected the land, because the grains came from this same land. The care and ethics of the farming practices were kept intact by the the baker's careful milling of the grains into flour, then crafted into loaves. All of this made for some really special bread.

This was all new to me. I began to relax into the daily grind of this life, these habits, these practices, these ideals. I didn't know it yet, but similar methods and ideals were making themself manifest back home. And soon I would be part of it.

Before Germany, I had never baked what I considered to be a good loaf of sourdough, let alone attempted something like a sourdough made with 100% rye flour. Here, I knew I was in good hands, as Enrique was a sourdough specialist. As a meisterbäker, he had trained under many other master bakers, each passing on their traditions and techniques.

As my work shifts came and went, I became very familiar with the features and layout of the bakery, including a shelf that held nothing but a line of small glass jars. Inside these jars were raisins, some of them soaking in water, some of them even gurgling in their liquid. After many shifts spent staring at them, I finally decided to ask Enrique what they were. His answer would prompt the start of my first successful sourdough culture, made by harvesting wild yeasts from dried raisin skins.

My previous attempts to start a sourdough culture at home had always involved mixing flour and water in a jar, and leaving it exposed to the air in different locations around my kitchen. It was exciting when these slurries showed signs of yeast activity, as evidenced by bubbles visible through the glass walls of the container. But these rogue cultures never really behaved reliably, and I was unsure as to why. I'd give up after an attempt or two of baking with it, often with lacklustre results. I'd let the culture age out of activity at the back of my fridge only to be discovered months later, its lid seized on, marked by a floating, ominous black liquid atop the sad-looking batter below. I didn't know there was another way, let alone a myriad of ways, to start sourdough cultures. But these little raisins in these little jars would soon become my go-to starter method.

Enrique had learned to make a sourdough culture from raisins thanks to a Japanese baker. The main sourdough culture for our bakery had been made in this manner, by soaking raisins in water and letting the yeasts living dormant on the skins of the dried grapes, activated by the presence of water, ferment the sugars from the raisins. Once bubbly and boozy-smelling, this liquid is then ready to be used to activate flour and become a sourdough culture. Enrique oversaw my first attempt to make a culture this way, a ferment I would tend to each day in the bakery. He taught me that the yeasts present on grape skins are excellent yeasts for making bread, and his devotion to this method was evident thanks to the tiny bottles on that shelf. He would even go through an annual process of fermenting new raisins, and when the moment was right, he would add this liquid to the existing sourdough culture with fresh flour, essentially boosting the power of the yeasts. These brews would then get labelled and shelved, with different vintages and eras of ferments on display. I became a part of his sourdough lineage that winter.

After the initial step of soaking the raisins, I would sniff my brew each time I entered the bakery. As with many things sourdough, Enrique taught me that using scent to interpret what is going on is essential. Since I hadn't done this before, I wasn't sure what to expect, but when a sweet and soft alcoholic scent started to emerge, Enrique let me know the mix was on its way to being ready. Alongside this emergent smell, the yeasts were waking up and starting to convert the sugars in the liquid to gas. I waited patiently for these bubbles, checking in on my jar each day. Finally, after some days of activity, Enrique let me know that the combination of active fizz with a gently boozy, sweet scent coming off the jar meant it was ready for the next phase. I strained out the raisins, left with an effervescent, clear brownish liquid that I lovingly added to a new jar that had a small amount of rye flour in the bottom. This moment is the *transfer*, when the precious grape yeasts from a water-based environment move into a floury one.

My daily sourdough task was to bring my baby out of the fridge, give it a feeding of flour with fresh water, turn it into a thick paste, and let it ripen during my shift in the warm bakery. During this week-long phase, the yeasts are being conditioned to the food available in the grain, adapting with each feeding. My feeding intervals slowed down, and after a week, the culture was established enough to be used in a bread recipe. I moved the culture to the farm with me, feeling confident enough to make a loaf of rye sourdough to share during the farm's brotessen with people who were slowly becoming friends.

THE RAISIN METHOD: STARTING A SOURDOUGH CULTURE

There are as many ways to start a sourdough culture as there are bread techniques out there. All of the methods are equally valid, and yield their own results, as well as their own fans. Essentially, the goal is to create and ferment a slurry of water and flour, cultivating yeasts that act as both agents of leavening and flavour along the way.

The yeasts that reside on grape skin happen to be very good for bread making, and thus a great way to inoculate your own sourdough culture with intentional, suitable yeasts. With the raisin method, you can have some confidence that the grape yeasts you are capturing will make good bread.

Clean hands, vessels, and tools are important for this fermentation, as is a warmish environment. Down the road you can repeat this process and refresh your mature culture by creating a new yeasty bubbly liquid and merging it with your existing culture during a flour feeding. Expect the process to take about 2 weeks, 1 week for your raisin liquid to get bubbly and ripe and 1 week to condition the yeasts to their new environment, flour.

You can choose any flour for your starter. I suggest rye flour because it makes for a vigorous and versatile culture that can be used for non-rye breads. Rye is an enzymatically rich grain, which means it is very capable of breaking down the carbohydrates in the flour, making the energy needed for the yeasts to do their thing readily available. Rye starters also keep longer in the fridge if you think you'll be more of a casual sourdough baker. If you mostly want to make wheat and white flour sourdoughs, I recommend using wheat as your starter flour.

Tools
250 ml jar

Ingredients
½ cup / 75 g organic raisins
180 ml / ¾ cup water
2 cups / approx. 240 g whole-grain flour

1. Sterilize the jar by scalding the lid and filling the jar with boiling water. Let the boiling water stand for at least 30 seconds, then discard.

2. Take ½ cup of raisins and place them in the jar with ¾ cup of water.

3. Put the lid on, not too tight, and store the jar in a place with the most consistently warm location. The top of your fridge is often a good spot.

4. Let the raisins ferment in the water: this will usually take about 1 week. If it takes longer, the risk of mould growth may increase and the space may not be warm enough. Generally, the fermentation will take longer in winter or in a colder space.

5. Look for signs of fermentation: the main observable change will be the arrival of bubbles. As the sugars in the grains are pulled into the water and start to ferment, the liquid will become effervescent. You may need to move the jar in order to notice the bubbles. Once you notice bubbles, smell it once a day, and watch for a yeasty and lightly alcoholic smell to emerge. Bubbles are a sure sign that yeasts are starting to become active in the forming starter.

6. After your mix has been vigorously bubbling for at least 1 day and for up to 1 week, strain off the liquid, and put the raisins aside or discard. When it is ready, it should be quite obviously gassy.

7. Choose what kind of grain you would like your starter to be made from. Have that whole-grain flour on hand. Add just enough flour, spoonful by spoonful, until the liquid becomes a thick paste. Put it in a new jar with a lid. Ideally you will have between ⅓ cup to ½ cup of this paste in your jar.

8. Let this sit for 12 hours at room temperature. Watch for gas activity by looking for bubbles in the starter slurry. If there is no sign of bubbles or expansion, the yeasts in the raisin liquid may have failed to transfer into the flour mix or weren't concentrated enough to populate the flour mix. Start over.

9. After the starter has sat for this 12-hour period, the yeasts will have had time to reproduce using the energy in the flour you have fed it. It will then benefit from a dormancy period, so put it in the fridge overnight or for the day, depending on your schedule.

10. Next, take your jar out of the fridge, discard about half of the starter and equal parts flour and water—making a thick paste again. Repeat this cycle of feeding, resting, refrigerating, and discarding a few times over the course of a few days. By doing this, you are conditioning the yeasts you have captured in your raisin brew to the flour you are inoculating.

11. After 4 days to 1 week with some feedings and rests, your starter is ready for bread making! Follow the care instructions below once you have established your culture.

NOTE: If a spot of mould shows up, carefully remove it with a clean spoon. If that is the end of it, carry on, but if mould shows up again you probably need to ditch this batch and start again, being careful to use clean hands and tools at each stage.

REFRESHING & MAINTAINING YOUR CULTURE

Once you take ownership of a culture, you are committing to caring for it. Think of it as a very low-maintenance pet. The more you are working with your culture, the happier it will be. Over the years, my culture has become used to my baking and care schedule. Yours likely will too. It is important to feed your culture *at least* once every 2 weeks if you want to be able to regularly come back to the sourdough culture and bake with it on demand. Some people feed theirs daily, or every few days, depending on their baking schedule. You will come to intuit what works best for you.

Feeding your starter is very simple. You simply remove it from the fridge and let it sit for 1 hour before adding flour. You should be doubling or tripling the volume of the total starter when you refresh it. Sometimes this means scooping out half or more of what is in your jar and throwing it away. An advantage of a regular baking routine, even if only once every 2 weeks, is that you don't waste as much flour keeping a healthy culture. The less you use your culture, the more you will have to discard before refreshing your culture in preparation to use it for baking.

So, to refresh your culture:

Ingredients
Your sourdough culture
35 –45 g / ¼–⅓ cup whole grain flour
30 –45 ml / 2–3 Tbsp room-temperature water

1. Remove culture from the fridge and let sit for a bit, 1 hour is good enough.

2. Remove anywhere from ½ to ¾ of the culture from the jar. (See Sourdough Discard Pancakes recipe on page 34.)

3. Add in the flour or more. Add in room temperature water. Mix until you have a thick paste or a loose dough ball, depending on the flour.

4. Let sit at room temperature for 4 hours. You should notice some gas activity in the jar. Return to fridge.

NOTE: If you see no reaction from the addition of flour and water after many hours, your starter may need to be left out for a full 12 hours. Refrigerate and then repeat these 'refresh' steps for a few days in a row until you notice life again in your starter.

SOURDOUGH DISCARD PANCAKES

When keeping a sourdough culture, there is what feels like unavoidable waste when it's time to feed or refresh it. Your temptation may be to add a bit of flour to the bulk of your existing culture, but when you bring it out of the fridge, most of the energy has been used up and it's likely more acidic than it should be. So rather than adding a tiny bit of flour to the existing culture in an effort to boost it, we want to remove about 75% of what we were storing and replace with that much more flour and water.

When this moment arises, here is a handy recipe I picked up on Instagram from badass chef and wrestler Jenn Crawford during deep lockdown, when one thing that *was* continuing was the sharing of food knowledge online, especially around sourdough bread making. This recipe asks for small amounts of seasonings to start, but feel free to experiment with what works best for you.

Ingredients
¼ tsp soy sauce
¼ tsp sesame oil
¼ tsp finely grated ginger
1 green onion, chopped
water
oil for frying

1. Place your leftover sourdough discard in a bowl. Season to taste with soy, sesame oil, and ginger. Then stir in some finely chopped scallions.

2. Start adding water to thin out the batter, 15 ml / 1 Tbsp or so at a time. Stir well after each water addition. Keep adding water a spoonful at a time until the batter reaches the consistency of a thin pancake batter.

3. Heat up a medium to large frying pan on medium heat. Once hot, add a splash of olive oil and a few drops of sesame oil. Pour the batter into the pan, in small circles, cooking for approximately 3 minutes per side.

TIP: You can also make bigger pancakes, more like crepes, and fold them over to serve with a high-quality soy sauce or a mix of soy, rice, or cider vinegar, and a touch of honey or maple syrup for dipping.

RYE
(Secale cereale)

Rye was the first grain I ever fell for. It's got a bold, sour, earthy essence that captured me early on when I would occasionally pick up imported pumpernickel. Those vacuum-preserved German loaves were crafted through a process that included days of fermentation, resulting in a natural, malty sweetness and almost cake-like texture. Even when making a relatively quick 100% rye sourdough (like the one on page 39), that earthy sweetness that comes from fermentation shines through in the finished loaf.

GEOGRAPHICAL ORIGIN & ERA OF EMERGENCE: Eastern Turkey, 10,000 BCE.

HISTORICAL IMPORTANCE: A highly resilient and adaptive plant, rye would often be the only cereal survivor during severe climate seasons. The vigour of rye fuelled various major population-growth eras in Europe from the early middle ages onward. Its adaptability and suitability for northern climates made it a survival crop for early North American colonizers, alongside First Nations–grown corn.

FLAVOUR NOTES: earthy, forest-floor, musky, molasses, chocolatey.

SPECIAL GRAIN FEATURES: Rye has some aggressive features, both as a plant and as a food. It has a distinct earthy flavour; it is lower in protein (gluten) than most other cereal grains; rye gluten is especially good at holding water, yet you won't get the same crumb structure as you would in wheat-based doughs. In the field, rye can be a vigorous and opportunistic plant. In bad growing years, rye often presents unintentionally in wheat and barley fields, being the only plant to make it to fruition.

When making sourdoughs, rye doughs give you a bit more leeway than wheat-based doughs. You can manipulate the fermentation times of your doughs to work in the time frame you have to make a loaf by using hotter or colder water without damaging or exhausting your starter or the structure of your loaf.

Sourdough rye loaves stay fresh for days and are mould resistant due to the acidity created

Maritime-grown, unmilled rye kernels and flour from Speerville.

Clockwise: rye flakes, stone-ground whole rye flour, kernels, and home-milled malted rye flour.

during fermentation. If stored right (in cooler temperatures and with time to breathe), a rye loaf can last up to 2 weeks.

CHALLENGES: Rye doughs tend to be sticky and can be harder to handle for a novice baker. Thankfully the more you work with it, the more you understand how it behaves. Rye flour is more potent than other grains during the process of fermentation, as the naturally present yeasts and bacteria feast on the sugars within the flour. Because of this, rye breads tend to be made only with sourdough as a leavener, rather than with commercial yeasts, which can lead to problems with timing, texture, and flavour.

The strong flavour of rye can need balancing, but it is in that balance that rye shows its strength, as it works so well with so many other flavours and textures, from cocoa in sweets to seeds in breads. Rye requires patience: the more rye there is in a loaf, the longer it takes for the crumb to set. Think about it as a curing time.

BEST USES: sourdough bread (adding rye to a bread recipe will help it retain moisture), cookie recipes, as well as cakes and quick breads where gluten is not key.

TRIVIA: Rye is prone to a fungus called Ergot, which can lead to a disease called ergotism. The disease is caused by various toxins produced by the fungus and causes various painful symptoms. One of the toxins produced by Ergot is lysergic acid, the principal compound found in LSD, and it has been theorized to be the cause of mass hysteria at various points in history.

100% Rye Sourdough

Makes 1 large loaf (using approx. 9 × 4–inch loaf pan)
Total dough weight: approx. 1150 g

Most breads made with 100% rye flour are sourdoughs. The distinct rise and texture found in sourdough ryes are thanks to its unique chemistry. The lactic acid and natural yeasts break down the proteins and carbohydrate elements in the flour, making a highly digestible loaf. Breads fermented with rye also produce a tart loaf ready for your favourite condiments, cheeses, etc. That acidity in the dough from fermentation also works to ward off moulds.

Proteins in the form of gluten are responsible for creating the sturdy structure of many wheat breads. The gluten strands stretch and hold carbon dioxide from the fermentation and create large bubbles and a more open crumb. However, the gluten proteins in rye are weaker than those in wheat. The starches and proteins in rye do a different, but similar job. They form a gel that holds onto the water in the dough, producing a moist loaf with a shelf life much longer than that of wheat breads.

Make sure that your starter is refreshed and ready to go before the next step (see page 33 for tips). If your starter has been idle for more than a week, refresh your sourdough culture the morning of, or the day prior, to mixing the overnight sponge. This dough involves minimal handling, a lot less than you may expect.

This bread is an excellent breakfast or sandwich bread. 100% rye is also fantastic when cut into triangles and served with a dollop of jam and a slice of a tasty cheese.

Equipment
dough scraper
large mixing bowl
scale (ideally)
large loaf pan **OR** Dutch oven
   (for a round loaf)

Ingredients
Sourdough sponge
150 g / scant 1¼ cups whole
   rye flour
150 ml / ⅔ cup room-temp water
20 g sourdough starter /
   approx. 1 Tbsp

Final Dough
500 g / approx. 4 cups rye flour
380 ml / 1⅓ cup lukewarm water
14g / 2 tsp salt

Hydration
82% (weight of water compared
   to grain)

1. MAKE THE SPONGE: The day before you want to bake the bread, prepare the overnight sponge by mixing the 150 g of rye flour and 150 g water with your refreshed sourdough culture. Cover and let rest overnight on the counter. The rest period should be no shorter than 8 hours and no longer than 14 hours.

continued...

Here Jess mixes the sponge, flour, and water by hand. Once well mixed, the dough ball is left to rest. Coming back to the dough, the ball has relaxed and expanded. It gets mixed by hand again before being transferred into the pan for the final proof.

2. MAKE THE FINAL DOUGH: The next day, mix the *overnight sponge* and all of the *final dough* ingredients together in a bowl by hand, spatula, or a mixer. Once you start mixing, it's best not to stop. The key to a good rye bread is making sure all of the ingredients are really well mixed, and the dough is totally homogeneous or uniform. Let the fully mixed dough rest for approximately 2 hours in a bowl, covered and in a warm location. (If it's cold out, you can preheat your oven to its lowest setting, turn it off, and put the unripe dough in it, covered.)

This rest period is the bulk fermentation phase where the sourdough yeasts are reproducing in the dough. You can check on the dough by watching for evidence that it is rising and becoming buoyant. You might notice this as bubbles forming close to the surface or cracks forming across the exposed part of the dough.

3. When doubled in size, grease a 9 × 4–inch loaf pan. With wet hands, scoop the dough up, gently cupping it while swiftly molding it into a log shape. Transfer the dough directly into the greased pan. Finally, dust the exposed top with a layer of rye flour (see image on the bottom of page 41 for an example). Let the dough rest for its final proof, approximately 45 to 90 minutes. Proofing the loaf in an

VARIATIONS

If you want to make a round loaf in a Dutch oven

1. Find a small mixing bowl and line it with a flour-dusted cloth or tea towel. (The dough will expand, so make sure the vessel is large enough for that.)

2. Round the ball by hand and place it in the bowl with the pinched dough pointed up, the smoothest side down. Proof in a warm location for 1 hour to 90 minutes. Halfway through this final proof, turn the oven on to 400°F and put an empty Dutch oven inside with the lid on.

3. Remove the now heated Dutch oven carefully with mitts, remove the lid, and carefully invert the round proofed dough into the Dutch oven. Score the top and quickly return the lid (with oven mitts) and place in the oven. Leave the lid on for 15 minutes then remove for the rest of the bake.

intentionally warm space will shorten the time it takes for the dough to do its final rise. When the dough has risen by at least a third in height and cracks form across the top, it's a good indicator that the proofing is nearing completion.

4. After the final proof, take your bread pan and score a straight line down the centre, about 1 cm deep, with a very sharp knife. Scoring can be flexible, so if your dough has proofed long enough it's become very wobbly, you may have to score more shallowly. Conversely, if you realize your loaf may not have proofed enough but you need to bake it anyway, you can score a bit deeper.

5. Bake the loaf for approximately 50 minutes in the middle of the oven. It will have come away slightly from the sides of the pan when done. If you have a thermometer, make sure the internal temperature has reached 200°F.

6. Let loaf cool for at least a few hours before cutting it to allow the crumb to set, otherwise you'll have a very gummy mess. Let it cure overnight at least, before sealing it in paper or plastic to extend freshness. Enjoy.

Transferring fermented rye dough into pan for final proof.

Finishing the loaf before final proof by sprinkling a dusting of rye flour on top.

Household Economies

'm not sure if any culture takes cake-making quite as seriously as Germans do. The daily ritual of kaffee und kuchen is an institution of German culture. Homes, businesses, and workplaces participate in this glorious ritual, making space for mid-afternoon coffee-and-cake-slice breaks, with every cafe around having its own special. Most holiday feasts don't start with dinner, they start with coffee and cake, followed by social time as guests rebuild their appetites for dinner.

Wandering into town for kafe und kuchen was a reliably sweet cure to the loneliness I felt in Germany. I'd try out the many different kinds of cake I had never encountered before, often indulging in a slice of a fruit laden-käsekuchen (cheesecake) or something involving chocolate and hazelnuts. Wishing I could share a slice with my mom or grandmother, the women from whom I had inherited my sweet tooth, I'd often write letters or record reflections in my travel journal, which was slowly filling up with recipes, names and anecdotes.

Kaffee und kuchen wasn't something only found in town; a mid-afternoon coffee break was a daily farm ritual, a welcome one during the cold days of winter farming. Though it usually didn't involve cake, sometimes the chilled and worn farm workers would be surprised with a decadent creation from the hauswirtshaft, also known as the home economics team: two women in charge of keeping us fed and sustaining our morale.

The hauswirtschaft team was responsible for more than just cake baking. They sourced, prepared, and served all of the meals to those who lived on the farm, maintained the kitchen gardens and chicken coops, preserved lots of farm-grown food, cured meats, made butter and cheese, kept on top of desserts, prevented food waste, and cleaned and maintained different areas of the farm. To be a permanent member of this highly specialized guild, one had to complete a three-year-long hauswirtshaft apprenticeship. By default, they also kept the farm spirit intact. Because of my experience catering, part of my farm duties involved making lunch, the only hot meal of the day. When it was my turn to make one of my "Canadian" lunches for the farm, I worked alongside the hauswirtschaft crew, wanting to show my skills while working at making friends with smiles, recipes, and whatever conversation I could muster with my growing vocabulary.

Cooking for the farm was another way I was able to share with my new farm family when language was still not an option.

Learning about a formal apprenticeship in homemaking and seeing this recognition of housework with its corresponding education system changed me and my understanding of careers. It validated and affirmed my desire to work with food professionally, while also showing me how the service of home making was a valid and important way to express care and sustain community. I often imagine what it would have been like to stay in Germany and pursue a formal hauswirtschaft apprenticeship, dedicating years of training to collaboratively learn the art of cooking, preserving, growing, and cleaning. Yes, I've said it—the art of cleaning. Oh, to have been trained on the standards of German cake making and kitchen garden design in the same course. This breadth of work reminded me of my grandmother and my aunts, the women who were always generously taking care of house business, amid the work of rearing the next generation.

As my winter in Germany unfolded, my meagre traveller's vocabulary expanded into the basics of everyday conversation, but with a growing niche in baking terminology. I enjoyed learning these words, and found German vocabulary surprisingly intuitive as an English speaker. As I was already loving the sounds of the language, baking words delighted me: ruhrig (stir), stauben (to dust), sauerteig (sourdough), zutaten (ingredients), rührschüssel (mixing bowl).

Daily exposure to bakeries and kitchens helped me pick up more and more of the language. At a certain point, I realized that cookbooks in another language were a lot easier than just about any other kind of writing. The topics were narrow, the language repetitive, the grammar simple. While I was still figuring out how to make friends with Germans in the afterhours, I was also spending time with different cookbooks I found on the farm, becoming familiar with the great expanse of cakes found within them. Where sourdough still presented many challenges and hadn't yet become intuitive to me, cakes just made sense. I'd made many and watched my grandmother make even more. They have an arguably simpler chemistry and process. I'd even sometimes make them on my days off. I liked bringing pleasure to the short winter days and the people I wanted to befriend on the farm.

I brought my recently expanded love of cake baking home with me, in the shape (or weight) of illicit butter and other ingredients I knew I couldn't find here. If I were to detail here the bulky provisions I smuggled back to Canada, you'd be shocked. This was still in the days when I would carry a "pack" a.k.a. a back breaker. It was so loaded I could barely pick it up. Surely overweight and somewhat illegal, it all made it home with me. This included about six heavy cookbooks I still peruse for pleasure reading, to use as learning material for language homework, to consult for inspiration, and bake from when I want to bring a little German cake magic into my life. I may not have done a great job at importing a routine kaffee und kuchen tradition, with its regimented times and near-daily cake consumption, but I still make fabulous German desserts for my community and my bakery customers, conjuring memories and the spirit of hauswirtshaft.

Double Chocolate Rye Cookies

Makes 24 large cookies

These cookies have been a customer favourite of the bakery for years, and rye cookies are a great way to slip some whole grains into the diets of selective kids or adults convinced they don't like whole-grain flours.

Rye pairs beautifully with cocoa, the darker the better. Because the cookie is so high in cocoa, using a darker, stronger-flavoured cocoa results in a flavour intensity that matches the punch of the rye. The high cocoa content of these cookies also contributes to the tender texture of the finished product.

These cookies can be made ahead of time—either by storing the dough balls in a sealed container in the fridge for up to 24 hours before baking or by freezing the freshly scooped dough balls for 2 to 3 months. If baking from frozen, make sure to let the dough balls thaw to the point where you can press them flat by hand.

1. Preheat the oven to 375°F / 180°C.*

2. Sift the dry ingredients—the rye flour, cocoa, baking powder, and salt—together into a bowl to eliminate any clumps. If any bran is left in your sifter, transfer it back with the other dry ingredients and whisk it in.

3. In a separate bowl, beat the butter and sugar together until you have a pale, whipped mix, about 1–2 minutes with a stand mixer or 2–4 minutes by hand.

4. Add the eggs one at a time, ensuring the first egg is well incorporated into the batter before adding the second one. Mix until the dough is fully homogenous, and has become fluffy and whipped again.

5. Using a firm spatula or a wide wooden spoon, add the dry mixed ingredients to the creamed sugar, eggs, and butter. Once the cookie batter is homogenous, add the chocolate chips and stir them in well.

continued...

Equipment
mixing bowls
sifter
whisk or beaters

Ingredients
Wet Mix
227 g / 1 cup soft salted or
    unsalted butter (extra soft if
    mixing by hand)
300 g / 1⅓ cups sugar
2 eggs (at room temperature if
    mixing by hand)

Dry Mix
300 g / 2½ cups dark rye flour
60 g / ½ cup dark cocoa powder
1 tsp baking powder
½ tsp salt
360 g / 2 cups your favourite
    chocolate chips

6. Spoon out heaping tablespoonfuls of the dough onto a cookie sheet: they should be around 55 grams each, or about 2 tablespoons worth of dough. Arrange 12 cookie balls per cookie sheet. Bake each tray for 14–16 minutes at 375°F.

7. If you have a cooling rack, transfer the cookies after they cool for about 10–15 minutes.

Once they have cooled, store the rye cookies in an airtight container for up to a week.

*A NOTE ON TIMING: These cookies don't need to go straight into the oven, and can often benefit from a period of rest in the fridge, either for a few hours or even overnight. They also freeze well as balls of dough, ready to be pulled out when needed.

VARIATIONS

· If you have a fancy salt at home (think fleur de sel, locally sourced sea salt) that you often don't know where to use, this recipe is a great place, as salt enhances the flavours of both the cocoa and rye. Sprinkle a modest amount of your flaky or coarse salt onto each cookie dough ball just prior to baking.
· For a holiday alternative, add a half-shot of cointreau or other orange-based liqueur to the dough, along with the finely grated or zested rind from half of an orange.

Left: Scooped rye chocolate cookie dough balls.

Right: A flaked sea salt garnish as soon as they come out of the oven.

Nutmeg Rye Blueberry Coffee Cake

Makes 1 cake

Coffee cakes are great to make with whole-grain flours because they don't rely on gluten for finished texture. This recipe would work just as well with a whole spelt or whole wheat flour, and that's what I love about it: it gives you opportunities to try various grains and flours and yet still results in a delicious cake. I make it most often with rye as it stays moist extra long and pairs nicely with the floral yet earthy flavour of blueberries.

In my home community of Charlotte County in New Brunswick, blueberries are a baking staple, and in my grandmother's home, nutmeg was a favourite spice. I feel close to her when I add nutmeg to my baking, even sometimes in savoury dishes (béchamel, anyone?). This cake is a whole-grain adaptation of one of hers, a buttery berry cake with a crunchy, sugary streusel layer that bakes on top. The original recipe was made with shortening, which does creates a very moist cake, though it doesn't contribute to the flavour as butter does.

Streusel toppings—made of butter and sugar and flour— are also perfect for exploring the flavours found in different whole grains.

I prefer baking this coffee cake in a bundt or tube cake pan but two smaller loaf pans or a round cake pan will work as well. Bake with fresh local blueberries and serve with a dollop of vanilla ice cream to create a perfect late summer treat.

continued...

Equipment

bundt / tube cake pan

> **OR** a 10-inch springform pan
> **OR** a 9 × 13–inch roasting dish

sturdy whisk or electric mixer

mixing bowls

Ingredients

Cake Batter

120 g / ½ cup salted butter, room temperature*, plus 1 tsp extra for greasing the pan

200 g / 1 cup sugar

270 g / 2¼ cup whole rye flour

2 tsp nutmeg

¼ tsp cardamom, cloves, or allspice

1 tsp baking soda

1 tsp baking powder

1 egg (room temperature if mixing by hand)

1 tsp vanilla or rum

185 g / ¾ cup plain yogurt (see: Variation for Dairy)

1½ cups blueberries**

* This dough can be mixed by hand, but make sure your butter is soft enough to be creamed easily into the sugar.

** If using frozen blueberries, toss them evenly in a separate bowl with 2 Tbsp of flour to prevent their colour from bleeding into your batter.

Streusel Topping

50 g / ¼ cup sugar

55g / ½ cup oats

55g / ¼ cup room temperature salted or unsalted butter

¼ tsp salt

1 Tbsp flour

½ tsp cinnamon

optional: 2 Tbsp chopped walnut or other nuts/seed such as almonds, hazelnuts, or poppyseeds

DIY BUTTERMILK

175 ml / ¾ cup whole milk or non-dairy milk

15 ml / 1 Tbsp lemon juice

Mix the two ingredients together and set aside at room temperature for at least 30 minutes and up to 1 hour. Use the same as you would the yogurt in the above recipe.

VARIATION FOR DAIRY

The yogurt in this cake tenderizes the crumb not just because of the moisture it provides, but also because of its inherent acidity. I am a fan of making my own buttermilk, the same way most commercial dairies do: by souring the milk with a little acid. If you are making a DIY buttermilk, start by mixing this before anything else.

1. Blend all of the streusel ingredients together in a bowl with a fork or by hand. Set aside.

2. Preheat the oven to 175°C / 350°F. Prep your baking dish by greasing it with 1 teaspoon of butter, and then flouring it by tilting and shaking 1 teaspoon of flour, coating the greased sides and bottom.

3. Mix your dry ingredients in another bowl. Whisk the flour, spices, baking soda, and baking powder together.

4. Cream the sugar and butter together in their own large mixing bowl. Continue creaming until the mix is noticeably paler and fluffier than when you started. Whisk the egg in completely and add the vanilla. Give it a final vigorous blend with your whisk or mixer to ensure your ingredients are well incorporated.

5. Using a spatula or wide spoon, gently fold approximately ⅓ of the dry ingredients into the wet mix. Once well incorporated, add ⅓ of your dairy. Alternate adding the dry, then the wet, about ⅓ of each every time, waiting for the mixture to be well incorporated before proceeding. When finished, gently fold in the blueberries.

6. Transfer the batter into your greased and floured cake pan. Level the top of the cake gently with the spatula. Evenly distribute the streusel mix overtop of the cake batter.

7. Bake in the oven at 175°C / 350°F for about 50 minutes. The streusel should be golden and crisped, and a toothpick should come out clean.

8. Let rest for at least 30 minutes before cutting. To remove the cake from a bundt pan, cover it with a plate. Tap the cake on the counter to loosen it a bit, then flip the pan while holding the plate tight to it. Remove the bundt pan and place a serving plate or cooling rack on top of it and flip once more to right the orientation of the cake. Let cool completely before storing.

Cardamom & Date Rye Cake

Makes 1 large (10-inch springform pan–sized) cake

Equipment
icing spatula (or dough scraper)
springform pan

Dry mix
210 g / 1⅔ cups of whole rye flour
1 tsp baking soda
1 tsp cinnamon
1 tsp ground cardamom

2 eggs
270 g / 1½ cups finely chopped
   dates
160 ml / ⅔ cup boiling water
5 ml / 1 tsp lemon juice
150 g / ⅔ cup room temperature
   salted butter (unsalted
   works too)
200 g / 1 cups sugar
75 g / ⅔ cup dark chocolate
   (65% to 75% cocoa solids),
   chopped finely

've been making this cake for so long I can't remember where the recipe came from. It is an adaptation of a recipe I found in a book of Scandinavian baking many years ago, but the title and the name of the author escape me. There is something about this recipe that speaks to me as a baker, and to my customers who form what I affectionately call "The Cult of Cardamom." So many Maritimers know the pleasing sweetness of dates in baked goods, and the rich comfort they bring. But this is not your grandmother's date cake. Cardamom and chocolate work so well together, and each of them work well with the intensity of rye, yielding what is probably one of the most popular cakes at my bakery. My editor, Simon, is such a big fan of it that just before we went to press, he convinced me to add it in.

1. Boil water and pour over the chopped dates, pressing the dates down to make sure they are submerged. Leave to soak for a 2–3 hours.

2. Mix and sift the dry ingredients together in a bowl. If any bran is left over from sifting, dump it back into the flour and whisk it back in.

3. Grease your springform or cake pan. Set aside. Preheat your oven to 175°C / 350°F.

4. Cream butter and sugar together by mixing with an electric mixer on medium until pale and fluffy. You can also do this by hand with a whisk for about 5 minutes.

5. Add eggs one at a time, mixing well after each integration.

6. Add the lemon juice to the date and water mix. Using a food processor, pulse for 10 seconds. If you don't have a processor, you can smash this mix with a potato masher.

7. Mix the dry ingredients into the creamed butter and eggs until combined, making sure to scrape the sides of the bowl to ensure everything is well blended together.

8. Add the dates into the batter until well combined.

9. Bake at 175°C / 350°F for 45 minutes.

10. As soon as the cake comes out of the oven, scatter the dark chocolate bits on top so they melt. Once fully melted, use a spatula to spread the dark chocolate over the top of the cake, pushing some to the edges as evenly as you can. Smooth the chocolate around the sides gently, as gravity pulls it down.

11. Let cool before slicing. Keeps well for 1 week. You are welcome.

Malted Grains

Malted grains are grains that have been soaked in water, activating certain flavourful enzymes in order to get them to sprout. After soaking, the grains are then dehydrated to make those enzymes go dormant. Once the malted grain meets water again—either in brewing beer or making bread dough—those enzymes are reactivated and create flavour through fermentation and the conversion of starches into sugars. As such, they are primary ingredients in beer and also one of my favourite sipping drinks: single malt whiskey.

The addition of malted flour to a bread recipe brings a special sweetness and depth of flavour out of the flour. Think of the malty character of digestive biscuits, certain wheat crackers, or even Ovaltine. It's also what brings a caramel-molasses type flavour that is common in many northern European rye bread recipes. When I visited a friend in Copenhagen a few years back, I was delighted to experience a whole new realm of rye flavour because of their use of malted flours, even though I had been working with them for years.

Here in Nova Scotia, I am able to source malted grains from a local malthouse that specializes in curing grain this way for brewers. Thankfully, more and more companies are malting and selling these grains and flours to customers, either directly or through online sources. You can even find websites that teach you to malt your own grains, a process which is easier than you think. And the best part? Malted grains are quite soft and can easily be milled in a spice grinder.

Nordic-style Malted Rye Bread

Makes 1 kg dough for a 9 × 4–inch bread pan

This bread recipe conjures the realm of texture and flavour I experienced while travelling in Denmark a few years ago. As this recipe contains rye in various states—from flakes to kernels to flour—it requires two separate bowls for pre-soaked ingredients, or *soakers*. In this case, soaked sunflower seeds, rye kernels, and the malted flour. By soaking some of the flour ahead of time, you unlock the natural sweetness from the grains by activating the flavourful enzymes within them.

The technique for this loaf involves a fermentation period in a mock-proofer you can create with boiling water and your oven. Giving rye sourdoughs a warm, moist environment will ensure that the sourdough yeasts from your culture will reproduce quickly so your loaf will rise in a comparable amount of time to a yeasted bread.

For a Danish meal experience, bake this loaf during spring. Take slices of cooled bread and spread them thick with unsalted butter, topping this dish off with layers of thinly sliced radish discs, fresh dill, a sprinkle of coarse salt, and a drizzle of schnapps if you are so inclined.

continued...

Rye sponge into rye flour.

Equipment
dough scraper
large mixing bowl
scale
large loaf pan **OR** Dutch oven
    (for a round loaf)
ovenproof dish, larger than your
    loaf pan.

Ingredients
Sourdough Sponge
40 g / ⅓ cup whole rye flour
100 g / 1 scant cup rye flakes
140 ml water / ½ cup + 1 Tbsp
    room-temperature water
20 g starter / 1 heaping Tbsp

Soakers
70 g / ½ cup sunflower seeds
70 g / ⅓ heaping cup rye kernels
100 g / ¾ cup malted rye flour*
60 ml water
* If you don't have malted flour,
    just use regular rye flour and
    proceed as directed.

Final Dough
180 g / 1½ cups rye flour
9 g salt
160–180 ml water / ⅔–¾ cup

Hydration
90%

1. Make sure that your starter is refreshed and ready to go before the next step. If your starter has been idle for more than a week, refresh your sourdough culture the morning of or day prior to mixing the overnight sponge (see Starter section on page 29 for more details).

2. **MAKE THE SPONGE:** The night (or 12 hours) before you want to make and bake your loaf, stir all of the sourdough sponge ingredients together in a bowl. Let it sit covered at room temperature. In the summer, sponges ferment quickly; in the winter, they move slower, so plan accordingly, but you're looking at an 8–14 hour fermentation time.

3. **MAKE YOUR SOAKERS:** Do this at least 2 hours prior to making your final dough. In a bowl, pour boiling water over the rye kernels and sunflower seeds. In a separate bowl, pour 60 ml of boiling water into the malted rye flour. After the kernels and seeds have soaked for at least 2 hours, strain them.

4. **MAKE THE DOUGH:** In a large bowl, combine the overnight sourdough sponge, the strained soaker, the malt soaker, the final 180 grams of flour, the water, and the salt. Work the dough by hand for a few minutes until everything is mixed well and the dough feels uniform. It will be sticky and easiest to knead directly in the bowl, with wet hands. You can use a stand mixer with the paddle attachment here, but it's always good to get your hands in there and get used to the feel of rye.

5. Let this dough rest for 90 minutes to 2 hours for the bulk fermentation.

6. Use a pastry brush or a tiny piece of paper towel to coat the inside of the loaf pan. Preheat the oven to 95°C / 200°F.

7. After the bulk fermentation, come back to your loaf. Watch for gas activity as an indicator as to how much your loaf has risen: the dough should have a buoyancy, with bubbles forming close to the surface or cracks forming across the exposed top part of the dough. With a very wet hand, knead the dough in the bowl for a minute, just enough to degas it.

8. Once you have degassed and lightly kneaded the still sticky loaf, transfer it into the loaf pan. With wet fingers or a dough scraper, smooth the top. Scatter the top with a mix of sunflower seeds and rye flakes. Take a sharp or serrated small knife and cut 3 diagonal lines going from side to side of the pan, about 1 cm deep.

9. Prepare a proofer for your oven: Bring a litre of water to a boil, either in a kettle or pot, and fill your ovenproof dish with the boiling water on the lowest rack in your oven. Place your loaf in the oven on the rack above the water. Close the door and leave for 1 hour to rise, and then after 1 hour, remove the loaf from the oven.

10. Preheat oven to 205°C / 400°F. Leave the ovenproof dish with water in the oven. It will reheat and steam as the oven heats up.

11. Once the oven has come to temperature, place your loaf pan in the middle of the oven and bake for 15 minutes. Remove the ovenproof water pan from the oven. Leave the loaf to bake for at least another 30 minutes, up to 45 minutes.

   You'll know your loaf is done when the internal temperature has reached 95°C / 200°F and it has coloured nicely. If you don't have a thermometer, watch for the loaf to pull away from the sides of the pan easily. You can even slip a dough scraper or metal flipper carefully down the inside of the pan to see if the dough has pulled away from the pan.

12. Let the rye bread rest for 12 hours or overnight before slicing, otherwise you'll end up with a very gummy loaf. To extend the shelf life of the loaf, let it air out for 24 hours before sealing in a container or plastic bag.

OATS
(Avena sativa)

Oats are featured throughout this book, but the oat recipes in this section explore oats as the substantive vessel that they are. Oats have a milky sweetness and a creaminess that is unparalleled. I love the mellow, buttery-leaning essence of oat-based baked goods.

Oats are easy to find and affordable. They are also available in various forms, such as oat groats (which is the entire kernel, including the bran, germ, and endosperm), steel-cut oats (groats that have been cut into small segments, irregular in shape but faster to cook than groats), rolled oats (steamed and pressed groats), as well as oat flour. Thankfully, cereal companies are beginning to market oat flour on a larger scale, making it easier to find. If you can't find oat flour on your own, you can always make a reasonable facsimile by pulsing oats in a food processor until fine. They can be made into so many different foods, even milks, yet there are few dishes as noble as oats simply boiled with water, butter, and a little salt and sweetness.

I love mixing oats with other whole-grain flours like spelt and buckwheat to make high-fibre, energy-dense baked goods. There are so many different cuts of oats available to consumers these days, meaning there is lots of room for home bakers to explore and experience how different ways of milling can create uniquely textured doughs. Beware: in baking there is a major difference between a flaked oat and a commonly milled style, steel-cut. (See Glossary.)

GEOGRAPHICAL ORIGIN & ERA OF EMERGENCE: Western Asia. There is evidence humans were foraging and hand-grinding wild oat seeds as far back as 30,000 years ago.

HISTORICAL IMPORTANCE: There are more steps involved in turning oats from a plant into food than there are with other grains in this book. To get oatmeal or oat flour, one must first harvest, thresh, clean, dry, sort, de-hull, steam/smoke, and then finally mill. Because of this complexity, the advancement of oat-milling technology spurred that of grain milling more generally. Prior to modern mills, oats used to be milled with a tool called a quern, a technology

Clockwise: Oats milled four ways: organic rolled oats, conventional oat flour, Speerville newfound oats, and homemade Vitamix oat flour.

more than 10,000 years old. Though the stone mills of today work very differently, they are still based on a similar principle, involving one stationary stone to hold the grain (the bed stone) and one moving stone to pulverize (the runner stone).

FLAVOUR: earthy sweet, creamy, delicate, silky, occasionally smoky.

SPECIAL FEATURES: Oats are considered a low-input grain, meaning they thrive in a variety of soils and don't require a lot of fertility for a good yield. Advantageous as a foodstuff, oats have a higher protein, fibre, and fat content relative to other common cereal grains. They are also richer in amino acids, which help the body digest and derive nutrients from plant foods. Oats thrive in rainy conditions, which is likely why they took hold in Scottish cuisine as early as they did, in the 5th century CE.

CHALLENGES: Having no gluten, ingredients like ground flax, eggs, or other starches are often added as a binder. Oats are milled in a myriad of ways and textures, which can make them behave differently than intended in recipes, especially when it comes to required soaking times and water absorption rates; if not balanced properly with moisture, oat recipes can turn out unpleasantly dry.

BEST USES: Oats are a great way to add whole-grain magic easily to bread; the baking texture is ideal for blending with glutinous flours in squares and biscuits.

TRIVIA: Oatmeal was one of the earliest breakfast cereals/foods to be packaged rather than sold in bulk and also subject to a major media campaign promoting it as a nutritious breakfast food.

Equipment

a large circular cookie cutter, or a wide-mouthed canning jar

Ingredients

½ tsp baking soda

½ cup hot tap or boiling water

300 g / 3 cups rolled oats (quick-cook will work as well)

240 g / 2 cups whole spelt or whole wheat flour

½ tsp salt

170 g / ¾ cup brown sugar

227 g / 1 cup cold butter (you can also use shortening, margarine, oil, or a blend)

VARIATIONS

- Instead of cutting the cakes into rounds, you can press the dough into an 8 × 8-inch square baking pan and deeply score the dough into squares just before putting it into the oven.
- Occasionally I spice the dough with nutmeg or cardamom, and I have even made a version where I replaced some of the oats with sunflower seeds.
- If you want to have them with soup or as a savoury baked good, cut out some of the sugar.
- The recipe also asks for brown sugar but will work well with white or another sugar that you like to bake with, such as coconut or date sugar.

Maritime Oatcakes

Makes 10–12 hearty cakes

Oatcakes were one of the first things I learned to make when I had my first home with friends. Like many baked goods that come out of diasporas, it is often a very regional recipe and highly adapted, having morphed since arriving in Atlantic Canada with Scottish settlers hundreds of years ago. This recipe is just sweet enough, thanks to the natural sweetness of the oats. Another virtue of this recipe is a long shelf life. I like to make these for camping or hiking and add M&Ms.

Maritime Oatcakes can be served with some cheddar and local jam to remind you of summer on the darkest days.

NOTE: I use butter in this recipe, but it can easily be made with any solid vegetable-based fat, margarine, or even a blend of fats. I often used to make a vegan version when I first started baking.

1. Preheat the oven to 400°F / 205°C.

2. Dissolve the baking soda in hot water, set aside. Using a knife, cut the butter into approximately 1 cm cubes.

3. Stir the oats, flour, salt, and sugar into a bowl. Cut the butter into this dry mix by using a pastry blender or a fork. Continue integrating until the butter is evenly broken up and distributed throughout the dry mix. Add the baking soda and water mixture to the dough.

4. Knead the dough by hand until the liquid is integrated and is looking and feeling homogenous. This should happen fairly quickly.

5. Turn out the dough onto a clean work surface sprinkled with oats. Pat the dough down flat and cut it into rounds, with a 3- to 4-inch diameter.

Space the oatcakes evenly on a large baking sheet.

Bake them at 400°F / 205°C for 10–12 minutes or until they turn golden. Cool for 10 minutes either on the pan or a cooling rack. Let cool completely before storing.

Oat Milk

Makes approximately 1 L

Contrary to popular belief, non-dairy milks are not new, fancy, or the ultimate in hipster chic. Making milks from legumes and nuts is an old practice. Almond milk was popularized in the Middle Ages by Catholics who would abstain from meat and meat products due to religious practices. Soy milk has been drunk in parts of Asia for hundreds of years. Oat milk, however, is relatively recent, having sprung up in the 1990s in Sweden. Oat milk is also much less invasive and water-intensive than almond or soy milks, which was one of the reasons it was developed.

Oat milks vary from brand to brand in terms of ingredients and sweetness. Some include stabilizers, such as vanilla, to prevent separation of flavours, so be conscious of that when using an oat milk as a substitute for dairy milk.

1. Start by rinsing the oats well in a fine-mesh strainer using cold water. This will rinse off some of the excess starch which will help create a silkier oat milk.

2. Add the rinsed oats and 4 cups of water to the blender. Add sweetener or salt here, if using.

3. Blend on a high speed for around 45 seconds or until the mixture is very well combined and the oats have broken down.

4. To finish the oat milk, pour your blended oat mix through a fine-mesh strainer or layered cheesecloth into a bowl or pitcher. Using a spatula, press the mix into the strainer to squeeze some residual liquids out. Stir before pouring into a clean, airtight container or jar. Add vanilla if using.

This oat milk will keep for 3–4 days. Make sure to shake it before opening, as it may have separated.

Use in smoothies, with cereal, or in baking recipes. You can also add lemon juice and let it stand for 30 minutes to make a dairy-free buttermilk (see page 48).

Equipment
blender
fine sieve

Ingredients
150g / 1 cup rolled oats
960 ml / 4 cups cool water
2 Tbsp liquid sweetener (more or less as desired)
½ tsp vanilla (optional)
pinch of salt

Land, Oatcakes, Family, and Cookbooks

The first version of this cookbook was a research project I designed and completed for grad school a few years ago. For that project, I took ten of my grandmother's recipes and created whole-grain adaptations of them.

I started the process by first baking her versions, then began integrating ingredients that differ from those my grandmother had access to. She would occasionally bake with whole wheat flour for bread, but she generally used all-purpose white flour for her recipes. I'm a grain lover, but truthfully, there are recipes I like to make at home to this day that use white flour. Through my recipe project, I became interested in tracing how her kitchen came to be stocked with the grains it did possess (wheat only!), when the kitchens of her Scottish ancestors would have been stocked with oats and probably even rye.

I'm a fifth-generation settler of the land we now call Canada. Not everyone calls it that, and for good reason. Names of places are complicated, especially when colonialism is involved. One of the reasons why you see names like Kjipuktuk/Halifax is an attempt to honour through naming the stated nature of the Peace and Friendship treaties, which we are still bound to though we live in violation of them. For me, pursuing a whole-grain future moves us away from industrial agriculture, which creates space to better care for the land, honouring more than a treaty.

As a white settler and someone who doesn't even know who or exactly where their European ancestors came from, my identity feels bound to Mi'kma'ki, though because this land is unceded, I live as an uninvited guest. I strive, even through the work I'm doing in this book, for a future where settlers honour the treaties created as frameworks for co-operative existence, rather than being a citizen of a nation who dominates through force. I imagine a regional grain economy like those I witnessed in Germany, and what local companies like Speerville creates through its network and distribution, making space for communities and new ways of working together that exist outside of the logic of domination in practices like spraying herbicide on a field of wheat to kill the plants simultaneously so they dry with total uniformity!

But I digress.

As far as I know, most, if not all, of my ancestors come from the British Isles. One way

I can trace my ancestors is through recipes and ingredients. Many of my various lines go back to Scotland. I feel an affinity for oats when eating and baking with them. They remind me, in a fairly ethereal way, of the homelands of my ancestors and help me feel like I can get to know them (and the land they would have farmed) for a moment. Working with recipes and preparing food is a way for me to make sense of my identity as a settler, one who is living here as an uninvited guest.

This is all to say: I am a baker and I particularly love bread baking. Bread and grain dishes hold deep cultural value as the bedrock of countless diets. And I love oatcakes.

Scottish Oatcakes

Makes 24 oatcakes

Equipment
rolling pin
food processor
1½ – 1¾ inch cookie cutter
(or equivalent sized tool like a
coffee scoop)

Ingredients
330 g / 3 cups of rolled oats, plus
more for dusting
¼ tsp salt
70 g / ⅓ cup unsalted or salted
butter (room temperature)
½ tsp baking soda
4 tbsp hot tap water

In Atlantic Canada, oatcakes are often placed in a "sweet" category of baked goods, sometimes filled with peanut butter or dipped in chocolate. Historically, oatcakes were actually closer to the savoury side of baking in Scottish cuisine, a vessel for butter, meats, and more.

This recipe allows the baker to grind their own oats at home, using nothing more than a food processor. By converting larger oat flakes—milled for oatmeal and cookies—into oatmeal, it allows home bakers to create cracker-like oatcakes. You can use any kind of flaked oat for this, just know that increased flake size will mean a longer time in the food processor to reach the fine consistency you are looking for. If you don't have a food processor but do have access to oat flour, you can use 1 ½ cups of oats and 1 ½ cups of oat flour.

These oatcakes are a tad more savoury than you might be used to. As such, they can be served with cheese, nut butter, or a tasty jam. You can also experiment with which solid fat you use; consider coconut oil or leftover bacon fat.

1. Mix the baking soda with the hot water.

2. Cut the butter into small cubes, about 1 cm x 1 cm. Set these both aside.

3. Process half of the rolled oats (1½ cups) in a food processor until they resemble a coarse, mealy flour. This should take at least 30 seconds.

4. In a large bowl, mix the remaining oat flakes with the newly-made oat flour and salt.

5. Preheat your oven to 190°C / 375°F.

6. Add the cubed butter to the dry mix bowl. Work it in by hand or with a pastry blender until the butter is well mixed but still pebbly.

7. Once the butter is evenly distributed through the oat mix, drizzle the hot water / baking soda mix overtop. Mix the water in, using a fork or your hands.

8. Press and knead the dough until it sticks together and feels like it can be rolled out.

9. Scatter some oats over the surface you will roll the batter out onto. Turn the dough onto the work surface and roll out with a rolling pin. Roll out the disk of dough to about ⅜-inch thickness. You can keep some flour handy to rub on the pin if the dough is sticking.

10. Find something in your kitchen that is about 1½–1¾ inch in diameter to use as a cookie cutter. Cut out as many rounds as you can from the sheet of dough you've rolled out. Gather the remnants and knead them back into a ball to roll out again and cut more.

11. Place on a baking sheet, leaving 3 cm / 1 inch between each. Bake for approximately 12–15 minutes, or until they have turned golden.

12. Cool completely on the cookie sheet or a cooling rack before transferring oatcakes onto a plate or container for storing. If you try to handle them while still warm, they can break easily. Store for up to 2 weeks in an airtight container.

Scoring raw Scottish Oatcakes.

Placing Scottish Oatcakes on a baking sheet.

The Rise of an Entrepreneur

Before I ever had a bakery, I had an enterprising spirit.

After some relatively slow-paced winter months on the Örkhof farm and a month in Berlin biking to my heart's content and going to German language school every morning, I moved on to Dottenfelderhof, a one-hundred-person farm community business where I would spend the next three months pushing my knowledge and love for bread further. Unlike the fairly chill vibe of Backstube Rosales, this bakery had four ovens (three of them wood-fired!) and a team of nine bakers, collectively creating thousands of loaves in a night. The shifts were intense, and I loved every minute of it.

I was a praktikantin (female who does practicum), so I worked in exchange for knowledge and unlimited sparkling water (able to choose between low, medium, and hard carbonation—if you know, you know). Another bonus: Falk, the head baker, offered in place of any monetary compensation for my six days a week of work in the bakery, the freedom to photocopy the bakery recipe book. Shocked and excited by this offer, one afternoon I carefully removed the precious binder from the bakery, slyly walked across the farm to the copy room, and went through the sleeve-protected (but still crusty) recipe printouts, each one scrawled with notes and scaled for a very large-scale operation. I copied many a recipe formula sheet, feeling an excitement about returning home and what kind of operation might be possible…

Once I returned to Canada from Germany, I was unsure what my future held. My homecoming was certainly full of possibilities, and I had a newfound passion for bakery life. Two friends of mine had bought a farm while I was overseas, and I was planning on living there that summer. We were going to "renovate" their newly purchased and dilapidated farmhouse, located on what the locals called the South Mountain, just outside of Wolfville in the Annapolis Valley.

That summer we were going to work the fallow fields. We had little experience, a workhorse we didn't really know how to work, and no barn. We needed income that first year, so despite the tough growing conditions of our weedy and stone-filled fields, we planted a market garden. Eventually naming ourselves Rocky Top Farm, we would drive in from the Annapolis Valley to Halifax once a week and set up an unsanctioned vending operation in the front yard of a friend's home on Agricola Street in Halifax's north end.

Since our produce offerings were generally sparse, I would stay inside on harvest day, trying my hand at making sourdough to sell. Each week, I turned our standard, if ancient, home oven into a small baker's oven. It was capable of turning out twenty loaves of rye sourdough in just a few hours with minimal smoke detector intrusions. Week after week, I would get out my calculator and notebook to scale down different Dottenfelderhof recipes, working through the stages of sourdough that I had practiced for months in Germany. Slowly, alongside trial and error, the modest intuition I had accumulated in Germany helped me create crusty, spongy, uniquely sour breads made with whole-grain flours only. And they would sell out, week after week, rain notwithstanding. This micro-bakery project was the beginning of my life as Jess Ross the Baker. It was also the first time anyone called me Chaos Ross...

Back at Rocky Top Farm, we lived on a budget. We would order dried goods from Speerville Mills, a New Brunswick grain mill and organic food distributor. Every six weeks or so, we would tack on a few 25-kilogram bags of organic rye, Red Fife, spelt, Kamut, and buckwheat flours to our regular order of rice and beans. The flours I received certainly felt different to the touch than I remembered, and they acted differently too, from the fermentation times to the degree of elasticity in the dough. Though I had done so in Germany, this was my first time working with whole grains on my own.

Jess holds a tray of her early recipe research experiments for *Rise*.
Photo by Farida Rady

Now that I had moved beyond standardized (read: all-purpose) white flour into the realm of whole-grain flours, I had come to the realization that white flour was universal and yet static, inert in flavour and character. I began to recognize that each mill, each grain, from each season, made a unique flour. There are so many reasons for this: everything from the weather, the conditions of storage, the variety of grain, the style of mill, the skill of the miller, and the freshness of the flour. Improvisation was always going to be a part of my home micro-bakery, but I was also learning the degree to which improvisation is fundamental to whole-grain sourdough baking.

Grain is a living thing, a food that grows in fields, and is impacted by the life it led before it was harvested, how it is handled afterwards, and how it's turned into flour. It grows, it changes, and so does the process of baking with it. Industrial food production doesn't really lend itself to improv. Its predictable, regulated, and homogenous nature are features of our most common, globally distributed ingredients. And I wasn't interested in baking like that, or in providing food for others like that.

As you might surmise, a small market garden and the profits from twenty loaves of breadwith some occasional cake slices—per week was not enough to sustain four young adults. It was a lean summer money-wise, but also often tense with the social dynamics of two friends running a farm on their new property while managing their two unpaid friend-helpers. So letting off some steam felt essential, and doing that at a local music festival that summer felt obvious. To make it feasible, my farm mate Mark and I hatched a plan to bake copious amounts of ready-to-eat M&M-studded oatcakes and sell them to our fellow festival goers. In my mind it was the perfect festival provision: inexpensive, filling, carb-loaded goodies suited to fuel periods of dancing to extended grooves. I was thoroughly convinced that every sun-stroked cutie would see the virtue of this superfood. Mark and I filled a large tote with two hundred oatcakes (baked in our overtaxed home oven, of course) and hauled them off to the festival for a weekend of outdoor dancing and illicit vending.

But they were hard to sell. A sign probably would have helped. Were we just reluctant to prioritize selling them once the party started? By Sunday we had only sold about fifty units. Had I miscalculated the mass-appeal of oatcakes? Did I really have what it takes to be an entrepreneur? In the end, we teamed up with a teen who claimed most of the profits in exchange for their youthful bravado, which they used to move the massive amount of oatcakes

we had left. Avoiding waste in the end, that now nearly empty bin of oatcakes left me feeling very satisfied though my pockets were empty. Even if I didn't bring enough tenacity to effectively solicit my wares, I had shown up with tongs, paper bags, and a small cash float. This was, after all, my summer of rogue bake sales and emergent entrepreneurship. On the slow journey home, with little sleep and a weekend of dancing outside having taken its toll, the small bounty of leftover oatcakes was a blessing. I would soon be ready to take my strange love of mass-producing good foods to the next level. But first, a nap.

As the summer wound down, the reality set in that a winter on the farm was not viable. I started to look ahead. Still feeling confused about career paths (and what to do with my anthropology degree), I followed my impulses and started a bakery. I had managed to establish some modest commercial baking practices as well as finding the recipes and techniques that worked best for me. I was also slowly piecing together that I didn't have to go to Germany to gain access to whole grains and the local food movement. I started to see that I could build a socially-engaged business by applying my new sourdough skills and by growing my connections to the local food system. That fall, I moved back to Kjipuktuk/Halifax, and Gold Island Bakery was born. The name Gold Island is a reference to a shimmering island utopia of good grain and craft baking, an idea and process that I wanted to manifest with my labour.

It didn't take much to find a perfect rental bakery space in the basement of a restaurant kitchen, a little spot called The Good Food Emporium. The Good Food Emporium was a legendary food-friends-and-dancing-community-institution kind of a restaurant. Rent was affordable. It included great company, hot coffee, and their famous sunflower seed chocolate chip cookies to fuel my not-yet-efficient workflow. Uninterested in a brick-and-mortar bakery, I wanted a low-overhead and flexible kind of business. Early on, I experimented with recipes and business models, including a labour-intensive (yet innovative!) bicycle-delivered sourdough bread and pie service. The subscription delivery model served me well in the chaotic early years of my bakery-owning life.

I baked every Tuesday afternoon and evening after launching my bicycle bread delivery service. Every two months I would launch a new prepaid subscription cycle, asking people to commit to receiving a weekly delivery of Gold Island Bakery goods that I would bake, pack up, and load onto my bike cart every Wednesday. Each delivery round had its own unique route; there were always new gardens to scope and huge hills to climb. Emotions ran high during this time, as there was no room to re-bake things if they failed, and sourdough loaves were a two-day process. Navigating the successes, and sometimes epic fails, of my baking endeavours required figuring out a collection of recipes and a scale of production that worked together in one shift, for just one aspiring baker to accomplish.

Pretty quickly it became clear that my weekly subscription was not enough to sustain me and perhaps not the most efficient way to run a bakery. The local Saturday market was at their quota of bakeries, so that didn't seem like an option. Luckily, my old boss, farmer Ted Hutten, was willing to sublet a corner of his existing market stall at Halifax's Brewery Market. The market manager accepted this, and on the first Saturday of 2010 I started vending there, exposing my whole-grain sourdoughs to a new audience all while selling raw apple cider

An earlier phase of *Rise* involved the author working to convert her grandmother's recipes into whole-grain adaptations while in school in Toronto. Jess was lucky to get to use Motherdough Mill & Bakery as her studio space. Each of the ten recipes she modified while there appear in this photo, and in this book! *Photo by Farida Rady*

for Ted in exchange for table rent. It would be almost a year before I could get my own table at the market.

I very slowly expanded my offerings, building my display up. I worked towards having my own space, though it was always hectic and never lucrative. I wasn't formally trained, and my previous experience as a caterer only carried me so far. I learned a lot by doing, while making sure I left space for adventure, all the while expanding my network of baker friends and mentors. I sought out bakeries across North America to help me cultivate a vision of what I wanted my own bakery production space to be like one day.

CORN
(Zea mays)

Corn is an incredibly special grain. Unlike the other cereal grains covered so far, corn is native to North America, and researchers have traced its cultivation as far back as 10,000 years ago in what is now Central Mexico. Over a millennia, corn has evolved expansively, with over 300 subspecies, each with hundreds of lineages and thousands of cultivars.

GEOGRAPHICAL ORIGIN & ERA OF EMERGENCE: Southern Mexico/Mesoamerica, around 8,000 BCE.

HISTORICAL IMPORTANCE: Corn has been an important food for many peoples from the western hemisphere over millennia. In most Indigenous cultures, it is deeply tied to spiritual practices and storytelling, reflecting the cycles of nature, and of life. Many sacred Indigenous agricultural relationships were tragically displaced as European colonialism reshaped local food systems. The impacts of this are still being felt today, even in our current global food system. My ancestors would have first experienced corn as newly arrived colonizers. Over time, corn, or maize, became a staple for European settlers, working its way into what would become American and Canadian cuisine. It's still an essential and celebrated ingredient in African American cuisine. Corn is also now deeply integrated into the global economy and industrial agriculture, grown for not only food but also fuel.

FLAVOUR: fruity sweet, floral, creamy, buttery, earthy.

SPECIAL FEATURES: Corn can be grown as far south as 50 degrees southern latitude and 50 degrees into the northern latitude and can live off as little as 10 inches of rain in a season and up to 400. This adaptability helped corn spread south 5,000 years ago, and later north into colder climates 2,000 years ago. European colonialism was responsible for a major change in how and where corn grew, dispersing it throughout many continents and cuisines of the world.

Clockwise from top left: Painted Mountain flint corn kernels, corn flour, followed by two distinct cornmeals, one much finer than the other.

CHALLENGES: Corn is a gluten-free grain and needs a leavener to create lift or texture. However, its flavour is unparalleled when blended with other grains in baking. The milling of corn varies widely from culture to culture, and even from brand to brand at your local grocer. Depending on where you source your cornmeal, you may need to adjust moisture levels to your doughs and batters, as some cornmeals may or may not include the cornstarch found within the grain, which is highly absorbent. If not balanced well with fats and liquids, corn baking can yield an undesirable dry crumbliness.

BEST USES: Corn is great for skillet baking or quick breads; makes an amazing contribution to both whole-grain and all-purpose bread doughs; when blended with all-purpose, whole wheat, or another sifted whole grain flour, it can be used in cookie and cake recipes.

TRIVIA: The interaction of technology and grains isn't just limited to the history of industrial agriculture. Humans have always created tools and processes to unlock the bound energy of dried cereals. One such process for corn is nixtamalization. This 4,500-year-old practice of soaking corn kernels with water and an alkaline (traditionally wood ash, which is a source of lime) allows nutrients and vitamins from the corn to be more easily absorbed by the body when eaten.

I didn't grow up eating a lot of corn as flour or as cornmeal, but I've been working with it now for more than ten years and I enjoy finding old corn recipes that shed light on the early interactions between Indigenous peoples and settlers through food.

Anadama Sourdough Bread

Makes 1 large loaf, or 2 smaller loaves

Equipment
dough scraper
large loaf pan or Dutch oven

Ingredients
Sourdough Sponge
100 g / ¾ cup whole wheat flour
80 ml room-temperature water
20g / 1 Tbsp ripe sourdough
    starter

Final Dough Scald
65 g / ⅓ cup + 1 Tbsp cornmeal
70 g / ⅔ cup oats
120 ml / ½ cup hot or boiling
    water

Final Dough
200 g / 1⅔ cup whole wheat flour
65 g / ½ cup whole rye flour
60 g / ¼ cup molasses
14 g / 2 tsp salt
100 ml water

Hydration
92%

I picked up my first loaf of anadama bread at an event in Maine called The Kneading Conference. It was made by a badass baker woman who ran a small whole-grain bakery near Portland. This recipe is inspired by that beautiful loaf, part of a lineage of northeastern settler brown bread recipes.

Recipes like this Anadama Sourdough Bread offer insight into the grain landscapes of our ancestors, telling stories about earlier times before there was even such a place as "Canada" and "America". Breads made only of wheat and eventually white flours became more common in the northeast as the colonial frontier spread west into the prairies. This meant the loss of Indigenous grain and grasslands, agricultural and culinary practices, as well as the long-standing displacement of Indigenous prairie peoples.

Many of what we now call "brown breads" would have traditionally been steamed, and would have contained a mix of corn, rye, oats, molasses (a common working-class sweetener), and coarse wheat from a rustic grist mill. Today's brown breads are mostly made with white flour breads, and are artificially browned with cocoa and molasses.

This bread benefits from rest periods which allow the flours to become more hydrated, the gluten more activated, and the dough overall easier to handle and knead by hand. This loaf has a tight but open crumb and a mellow molasses taste. This lightly sweet loaf can be topped with butter and a drizzle of molasses when fresh, and gives sandwiches a sweet edge.

Anadama Sourdough Bread baked in a Dutch oven.

1. Ensure that your sourdough culture from the fridge is not spent of energy. If necessary, refresh your sourdough culture at least the morning prior to mixing the overnight sponge.

2. The day before you want to bake the bread, mix the starter whole wheat flour and room-temperature water with your sourdough culture. Cover and let rest overnight on the counter.

3. The next morning, mix the cornmeal and the and oats together in a large bowl. Scald the cornmeal and oat mixture by pouring the 120 ml of hot or boiling water over them and stirring well. Let this rest and cool for at least 30 minutes, otherwise you risk damaging the yeasts in your sourdough.

continued...

Partially fermented Anadama dough, about to be folded during bulk fermentation.

Hand-working the dough to develop gluten intermittently during the fermentation.

Sometimes when it feels too sticky and Jess doesn't want to add any more flour, she prefers working the dough in the bowl with wet hands and without flour instead.

4. Mix the Sourdough Sponge and the Final Dough ingredients *except* the salt in a bowl by hand or a mixer. It will be very sticky at first but keep mixing until it forms a ball. Let the dough rest for 30 minutes.

5. Next, add the *final dough scald* and salt. Mix well, until the dough starts to become cohesive and well-mixed. Let rest for 15 minutes.

6. *If using a dough mixer,* mix for 5 minutes on medium-low, watching that the dough starts to more easily come away from the walls of the bowl as it mixes. The dough should start to become smoother, sticking less to the sides of the bowl.

If mixing by hand, keep water nearby for your hands, to ease the stickiness of the dough to your hands. Don't worry if the dough seems a bit wet, keep mixing it in the bowl for a bit before transferring it onto a floured surface to knead. As you work the dough, it should start to feel more elastic, gaining an ability to be kneaded tight, into a ball that holds some shape, after 6–10 minutes of kneading.

7. Place the dough in a bowl. Take about 1 teaspoon of butter or another fat. Warm it in your hands and then gently rub it over the top of the dough, and finally drape the bowl with a tea towel or a makeshift lid. Leave it to rise for 90 minutes, up to 2 hours for the bulk fermentation.

8. After the bulk fermentation, turn the dough onto a floured work surface. Trying to touch only the floured edges, with floured hands, fold the edges of the dough in on itself, left edge to the centre, right edge to the centre, and then top to centre, and bottom to centre. This helps to work the gluten and bring tension back to the bread dough. Return to bowl and cover. Let rest for 45 minutes to 1 hour.

9. At this point, you can make one large loaf or two smaller loaves. Prepare your bread pan or Dutch oven.

FOR A BREAD PAN: Grease your pan and dust with a little flour. Take the kneaded dough ball and flatten it with your fingers. At 10 and 2 o'clock on your dough circle, fold the outside edges closest to your left and right hands into the middle, and then, from the top, tightly roll the rectangular dough disk into a log. Place it in a pan with the seam down.

FOR A DUTCH OVEN: Find a soup bowl or smaller mixing bowl and line it with a flour-dusted cloth or tea towel. It will expand, so make sure the proofing vessel is large enough for that. Round the ball by hand and place it in the bowl with the pinched dough pointed up, the smoothest side down.

10. Proof in a warm location for 1 hour. Halfway through this final proof, preheat the oven to 205°C / 400°F. If using a Dutch oven, place the empty Dutch oven inside with the lid on.

11. After this final proof, take your bread pans and score a few lines or a design along the length of the bread with your sharpest knife.

If you are baking the bread in a Dutch oven, remove it from the oven with mitts, remove the lid, and carefully invert the round proofed dough into the Dutch oven. Score the top and quickly return the lid (with oven mitts) and place in the oven. Leave the lid on for 15 minutes then remove for the rest of the bake.

Bake for 50 minutes to 1 hour in the middle of the oven. If you have a thermometer, make sure the internal temperature has reached 95°C / 200°F.

Let cool for 3–4 hours, to allow the crumb to set and some moisture to evaporate. Let cure at least overnight before sealing in plastic to extend freshness.

Orange Blossom Corn Cake

Makes 1 large springform cake

Equipment
9- or 10-inch springform pan
whisk or electric mixer

Ingredients
240 g / 2 cups corn flour
1½ tsp baking powder
¾ tsp baking soda
½ tsp salt
175g / ¾ cup sugar
3 room-temperature eggs,
    separated into yolks and
    whites
1 tsp cream of tartar
170 g / ¾ cup room-temperature
    butter (softened further if
    mixing by hand)
15 ml / 1 Tbsp orange blossom
    water
15 ml / 1 Tbsp honey
1 tsp orange zest
optional: 12–14 individual small
    berries or 6 strawberries,
    sliced and set on top of the
    cake

This light and fresh cake uses fine corn flour (not cornmeal) to produce a delicate but flavourful crumb. Part of its lightness comes from the orange blossom water and honey, two floral flavours that build on the natural sweetness of the corn. The orange blossom water is also an homage to the Arab world, a region where so many of our globally beloved grains have come from, including wheat.

This recipe technique is similar to a sponge cake known as a genoise, where the whites of eggs are whipped into a stiff meringue and delicately blended in during the final step of the cake mixing. The stiffened egg whites give some extra stability and loft to this gluten-free cake recipe (See note on gluten-free corn on page 75). Cornmeal *can* work with this recipe, but it will not be as delicate, and may sink in the middle. However, don't let aesthetics deter you. Corn is delicious, as this recipe will show you.

This cake can be made in a springform pan or a rectangular roasting dish if you'd rather cut squares than triangular slices. The cake also pairs well with berries, either gently pressed into the top of the cake just prior to baking, or served with some lightly sweetened stewed fruit as accompaniment. Whipped cream or a similar whip adds a nice textural contrast to the slight coarseness of the corn cake. Best served fresh.

1. Mix the corn flour, baking powder, baking soda, and salt in a bowl. This is your dry mix. Set aside.

2. Grease your springform pan. Preheat your oven to 170°C / 350°F.

3. In a large bowl, whisk the butter and sugar until the butter begins to pale in colour.

4. Add the egg yolks one at a time, waiting for each yolk to be fully blended before adding the next one. Continue to mix until well incorporated.

5. Take the sugar-yolk mix and add the orange blossom water, orange zest, and honey. Combine thoroughly.

6. Whisk the egg whites and cream of tartar in another bowl. Continue to whisk, incorporating air into the egg whites, until you get to the stiff peak stage. (You know you're there when the egg whites have become white and frothy, and can be shaped into a peak without collapsing.

7. Into the sugar-yolk mix, add ½ of the dry mix and stir with a spatula until mostly blended in. Then add approximately ⅓ of the egg whites and gently but swiftly integrate them. Continue to alternate integrating the dry mix into the batter, followed by the egg whites, and mix everything just until combined.

8. Pour the cake batter into a greased springform pan. Smooth the top gently. If using sliced strawberries or other fruit, gently place and space out on top of the smoothed batter.

9. Bake cake at 350°F for about 30 minutes. If your cake is browning too quickly, reduce the heat. It is important for the cake to set well before removing from the oven, even when it looks done.

10. Let cool for about 1 hour before releasing the springform pan. If the cake doesn't want to release from the sides, snap the springform shut again and take a butter knife and gently go around the edge of the cake. Enjoy!

A NOTE ON MIXING: Part of my baking ethos is that my recipes should be able to be duplicated—even without fancy equipment. In the case of this recipe, mixing by hand does test one's whisking stamina. Make sure you are whisking in the most ergonomic way possible (sometimes I stand while holding the bowl lowered in the air with one hand, arms extended, relaxed and dropped, whisking with the other hand). When doing sensitive cake work like folding stiff egg whites into a batter, I like to use my hand. There's no tool that can as effectively and delicately blend a sponge cake when you are adding the whites. You want to preserve as much of the volume of the egg whites as possible. However, a stiff spatula also works.

VARIATIONS

This cake recipe works very well many other flours, as it does not depend on gluten development for structure or lift.

A NOTE ON GLUTEN-FREE: Although corn is naturally gluten-free, it isn't always milled in a location that can guarantee it is free from gluten. Check the label before proceeding if gluten intolerance is an issue.

Baba au Rhum with Tahini Caramel

Makes 12 mini babas or 1 bundt baba

Equipment
muffin tin or bundt / tube pan

Ingredients

Cake Dough
60 ml / ¼ cup warm water

2 tsp dry active yeast

⅛ tsp salt

25 g / 2 Tbsp sugar

60 ml / ¼ cup melted butter
(should be warm/tepid and
still liquid but not hot)

2 eggs

175g / 1 cup plus 3 Tbsp of
white flour

60 g / ½ cup corn flour or fine
cornmeal

Rum Syrup
240 ml / 1 cup water

200 g / 1 cup of granulated sugar

240 ml / 1 cup of cold water

120 ml / ½ cup of rum

Tahini Caramel
30 g / 2 Tbsp butter
(or coconut oil)

60 ml / ¼ cup stirred tahini

60 ml / ¼ cup maple syrup

½ tsp sea salt (or a good
opportunity to use fancy salt if
you have some on hand)

Although I bake with whole grains at home, on occasion a touch of white or all-purpose comes in handy when I am looking to bake or teach people how to integrate whole grains their baking, a stepping stone if you will. When I was just establishing myself as a baker, I encountered this dessert when an old roommate's friend brought it over for us to share. I forgot about it for years until it flashed in my memory randomly one day. As such, I've introduced a portion of corn flour into the recipe because I love pairing corn with molasses (rum is made from molasses!). Both corn and spiced rum are earthy in their sweetness, with corn becoming nutty when baked, and the rum holding bittersweet, dark malty notes.

Corn and rum are foods with heavy histories, both a part of the British colonial trade route, where enslaved peoples, Caribbean sugar, and Maritime rum were moved on the same ships travelling between England, west Africa, the Caribbean and the northeast Atlantic. With a little digging, it's easy to see recipes as time capsules of sorts.

I honed my technique for baba au rhum watching a Julia Child video on YouTube. Tahini caramel was introduced to me by a roommate who would surprise me occasionally with a casual fine dining experience at home after a long day, often including a dessert that would be served with this tahini caramel. The baba is delicious on its own, but serving it with this nutty vegan caramel will make your friends and family feel special.

1. Whisk the water, yeast, and sugar in a large bowl together and let sit for 5–10 minutes. Whisk in the eggs, then the melted butter.

2. Add the all-purpose flour, cornmeal, and salt and mix in the bowl, stirring everything together. Work the dough in the bowl with your hands, kneading it persistently, until it starts to become less sticky. (It will be very sticky at first; keep going).

3. Once the dough is starting to smooth out, take it out of the bowl with one hand and slap it down into the bowl, then take it out again and slap it in the bowl once more (this is the Julia Child kneading method for a yeasted baba dough). Do this for a while until the dough starts to pull away from the bowl more cleanly, without leaving much behind. Then transfer it to a lightly-flour-dusted surface and knead into a ball.

4. For the first rise of the dough, place it in a bowl and cover it with a makeshift lid. If your kitchen is cool, warm your oven to its lowest setting and turn it off once preheated. Then place the covered proofing bowl into the warm space.

continued...

Dry active yeast proofing.

Demonstrating the Julia Child technique with raw Baba au Rhum dough.

Jess rolling out the baba ring while gently pressing down to lengthen the dough as she rolls.

Baba au Rhum dough ring in the pan before it has risen.

5. Let rise until about doubled in size. When you push your finger into the dough and it doesn't spring back at you, it's ready. Once your dough is here, punch it down and knead it back into a ball. Let it rest for 1 minute then use both hands to press and roll the dough ball into a log. Here, you are gently pressing down with your fingers while moving your hands forward and back, spreading your fingers as you press.

6. *If you are making mini babas,* roll out the dough so that you can easily cut 12 chunks of dough. You can use small cylindrical baking moulds or a muffin tin. Divide the length of dough into 12 equal pieces with a knife or scissors. Gently reshape them in your hands as you move them into each muffin cup.

   For one large bundt baba, roll the dough long enough so that it will fit in your bundt or tube pan where one end can overlap onto the other to complete a ring. Use your hands to work this section of the ring together, trying to dissolve the seams where the two ends meet. Once joined and smoothed, place the ring in the buttered pan.

7. Let the dough rise in a warm location for 30–50 minutes. (Note: The mini babas have proofed enough when they have risen to the top edges of the muffin cup.)

8. Preheat your oven to 190°C / 375°F.

8. Once proofed and ready to bake, place in an oven. Bake the bundt for approximately 18 minutes and the baby babas for 15 minutes. They should become golden.

9. Remove from the oven and let cool for 10–15 minutes before turning out onto a cooling rack or other surface.

If you made a large bundt baba, use a fork to sparingly perforate the sides.

If you made mini babas, take a fork and perforate the sides gently as you rotate the baby baba in your hand.

10. While the babas are cooling, make the rum syrup. In a medium saucepan, add water and sugar. Bring to a boil, stirring occasionally to help the sugar dissolve. Remove from heat once brought to a boil.

Next, add the cold water to cool and thin the syrup. Stir in the rum.

11. At this point, your baba has ideally cooled off some. It should be warm or tepid but not hot.

Soak the baba in the syrup for 30 minutes. You can pour all of the syrup directly into the bundt pan and then place the baba ring back in the pan with the syrup. For individual babas, use a roasting pan or similarly sized vessel to soak all twelve at once. Spoon or baste the syrup over the babas and rotate them a couple of times during their 30-minute soak.

12. After the soaking time is complete, drain the baba for 30 minutes.

13. While the baba is draining, make the Tahini Caramel. Using medium-low heat, melt the butter in a pan. Once the butter is melted, add the tahini and maple syrup. Let the mixture bubble and thicken for 1–2 minutes, stirring constantly to ensure the caramel doesn't burn. Remove pan from heat and finish with ½ tsp of salt.

Plate the bundt baba or baby babas and finish by drizzling the tahini caramel overtop. Enjoy!

NOTE: You can make this baba ahead of time and freeze it *before* you soak it. Wait to make the rum syrup and caramel until the day you want to serve it. Thaw the baba cake to room temperature before soaking in syrup.

To Come to Know

Before I understood the potential of whole grains in my own region, I had to go through the process of coming to know their history here.

Within the first year of my young career as an informally taught baker, I met Doug Brown. Doug was an emissary for locally-grown and -milled whole-grain flours. Alongside running his own whole-grain bakery, Doug worked as a sales rep for Speerville Mills, a mill and wholesale vendor of grains and flours in New Brunswick. The mill had recently changed hands and under the new local management it was growing and trying to reach new audiences. Doug was a knowledgeable baker who worked as their charismatic ambassador. The year I returned from Germany, Doug had been invited to teach a workshop on whole-grain pastries at The Kneading Conference, an annual grain conference that takes place in Skowhegan, Maine. We had connected the same summer, as I was a new Speerville customer, and, lucky me, Doug invited me to join him at the conference.

The Kneading Conference is a gathering for passionate local grain farmers, bakers, and millers from all over North America, and even

the world. It is an incredibly generative learning space. I've met baker friends there, learned techniques, and tasted flavours and textures I couldn't have imagined were possible in any kind of baking. It's also where I came to understand how prominent wood-fired ovens are in North America. The conference fair grounds were a constellation of mobile wood-fired ovens, each brick oven set up to host one of the various workshops happening over the three-day gathering. Some of the ovens were on wheels, while others were in the early stages of being built for educational purposes, accented by piles of bricks and buckets of mortar and mud here and there.

The Kneading Conference didn't sprout from just anywhere, it is the culmination of cultural and agricultural reclamation, centred around whole-grain sourdoughs and wood-fired ovens. The conference evolved out of a gathering of bakers in the 1990s, led by a galvanizing figure of the craft baking movement, Alan Scott. After his passing in 2004, the gathering went dormant for a while and when it emerged again, it became a public, movement-building event, named The Kneading Conference. Recent decades have seen a steady, slow return of craft baking, disseminated through articles, social media posts, and bakers selling increasingly interesting and previously unseen baking methods from around the world. Not to mention more and more conferences like The Kneading Conference are happening all over North America and Europe.

The conference happens on exhibition grounds that are designed to host rural events like 4-H competitions and livestock showcases. But on this particular weekend, the paved grounds and grassy zones were for the baker nerds among us, the arena held for keynotes and gatherings, the bleachers for night baker beers. I had no expectations for this trip, and certainly didn't expect to find a community who felt like they were my people: people who were planting, nurturing, and harvesting the many seeds of regional grain economies. Some of the workshops were what you may expect at a conference, like the Perfect Pizza Crust class taught by a baker from America's Test Kitchen. But some of them were radical, designed to equip passionate bakers with the knowledge they needed to work with the same wild whole-grain flours I was experimenting with back home. I was learning not only about how to work with local whole grains, but *why* whole grains are important to communities. The environment of the conference fed the food activist in me, with ideas germinating in new and exciting ways.

That year at the conference, I was tenting amongst a little community of participants in one corner of the grounds. As is typical for me at most conferences I attend, there was an awkward social element to it. Nerves aside, I could see the rare opportunity of this specialized gathering. Since I was staying on-site, I put myself out there, hanging out with some of the extended workshop crews, like the production baking workshop led by Richard Miscovich and the weekend-long clay- and brick-oven–building workshops led by Pat Manley. The oven builders were busy from breakfast to dusk, working within an ambitious timespan to make a wood-fired oven from scratch. Many of the people I socialized with after-hours were bakery owners and other actors in the movement. There were brilliant bakers with fascinating backstories, activist organic farmers sharing the harms of industrialized wheat farming and offering lessons about small-to-mid-sized grain growing, and of course there were millers making their case for why their trade couldn't be left out of the regional grain revolution. A revolution we all wanted to be a part of by the time the conference concluded.

One of these millers was Roger Jansen. Roger was an accomplished old-timer, an elder who held decades of wisdom and stories from what felt like a distant past. He was something of a back-to-the-lander, at least insofar as his epic skill set. That and raising his kids on a commune in Vermont in the 1970s. Roger had worked as a bike engineer for Peugeot in France. With his engineering skills, he went on to spend some years building grain mills for Meadows Mills in North Carolina. When I met him in 2009 he was also a prolific potter now, in his eighties.

Part of Roger's life's work was keeping the stories of grain mills in North America alive. During the 1800s there had been many companies that made mills, to support the demand at a time when every emerging settler community and many Indigenous communities had their own mills. By the time I met him that year, Meadows Mills was the only company in North America that was still making stone-ground flour mills. Most of the bakeries across North America with in-house flour mills were ordering them from Europe. Roger and I got to talking after one of the conference events. I was doing a lot of listening, learning about Roger's mission, and coming to understand why it was not okay that milling was something of a lost craft in North America. Kansas State University was the only place that had a training program, and even that was geared to train industrial white-flour millers. This meant that industrial scale was the only scale being taught, and there was no room being made for millers who cared about producing and milling quality whole grains and whole-grain flours.

Roger wasn't only preaching about milling, he was also a devotee to a specific baking tradition, a whole wheat sourdough method hailing from Belgium, called desem. His son Larry was a desem baker in northern California, where together they had built many ovens and mills for themselves, as well as flour mills to sell. Never having heard of the desem tradition before, Roger revealed a creased photocopied article, "The Staff of Life," from 1979, telling the story of Baldwin Hills Bakery, a rare whole-grain bakery from that era. The bakers in this story were holdouts of a bread tradition teetering on the brink. Having recently returned from Germany where I had become steeped in traditional baking practices, knowledge, and daily eating habits, I was fascinated by this, as well as the fact that other people were seemingly just as devoted as I felt towards all things grain-related. In fact the whole conference was teeming with people just like me.

To keep the conversation going, Roger invited me to run an errand with him that evening. He was preparing to teach a workshop on stone-dressing, the skill of sharpening the millstones—the stationary bottom bed stone and the spinning top runner stone that work in tandem to grind grain kernels into flours. With all the time in the world that evening and a desire to see some of the surrounding area, I hopped in the car and we set off to Albie Barden's place for some tools. Albie is one of the founders of, and a father figure to, The Kneading Conference. Albie and his son build wood-fired ovens for a living and many of the mobile ovens on-site were crafted by them. His presence during the conference was practical, but also spiritual.

Albie had a message to share about corn, specifically flint corn. Flint corn has a hard exterior layer, is often multicoloured and drought resistant. For some years Albie had been a part of a seed project, growing and saving seed passed on to him by Kanien'kehá:ka corn keeper Steve McComber. Kanien'kehá:ka is the traditional name of the Mohawk. The word itself translates to "People of the Flint." Albie was fond of a particular flint corn from the Haudenosaunee called Darwin John. This flint is native to the northeast, its name coming from the Onödowá'ga:/Seneca Elder and seed steward who was responsible for disseminating that corn.

I knew corn was Indigenous to the Americas, but I wasn't aware that there were corn varieties grown for millennia in the part of North America I consider home. Short-season flint corns like Darwin John have long been farmed on the banks of the Kaniatarowanenneh/ St. Lawrence River, challenging the mainstream assumption that Indigenous people didn't farm. It was this kind of rhetoric that was often used by settlers to justify taking land during the settling and colonization of this continent. Agricultural histories such as this one have been used to bolster an invented binary of "civilized" settler and "backwards" native, reinforcing a logic of domination.

I first learned from Albie that corn also played a part in the early history of contact between First Nations people and European colonizers. Corn was a central crop in food systems of the northeastern Indigenous peoples of the Haudenosaunee and Wabanaki Confederacies, territory that The Kneading Conference was taking place on, centuries later. In reality, the growing practices and stored corn of people like the Penawapskewi/ Penobscot in Maine helped keep colonizers alive when they arrived here, under-resourced and unable to work the land. Indigenous agricultural knowledge stabilized setter communities, who over time took over the land First Nations had been stewards of for countless generations. History lessons like these are a political part of the process of coming to know, of unlearning what you thought you knew, even about grains.

I learned some of this food history for the first time that summer, from Albie. I would become a part of that seed propagation project and am now also a steward of Darwin John corn. Despite the absence of Indigenous peoples at the gathering—an issue with the local food movement in general—I left the conference with my twelve corn kernels and a new awareness of the role of corn in the history of settler colonization in the northeast.

When we said goodbye at the end of the conference, Roger handed me his number and a few more baking articles to mull over. I tucked them away and drove off with Doug and his kids, hooked even more whole grains. Over time, these lessons helped me to see baking as a craft where I could help make the food system more robust, more environmentally friendly, and as a space to work on redefining the settler relationship to land and agriculture.

The next summer, just before I headed to The Kneading Conference again, I planted my first patch of Darwin John corn. That fall, I harvested my modest crop (what the racoons left behind, anyway) and let those ears of corn dry. I now had hundreds of kernels to grow out again for next year, to help continue the cycle. Maintaining relationships with grains at the plant stage helps me appreciate the countless generations of seed savers that keep unique grains vital and available to be grown by future generations.

SPELT
(Triticum spelta)

Spelt is an amazing grain to start with if you want to branch out from all-purpose or whole wheat flours. It has a mild flavour compared to whole wheat flours, featuring the nuttiness of other cereal grains, but is quite soft in character and mildly sweet.

Like wheat, the stickiness of whole grain spelt doughs slowly fades into a smooth, touchable dough. One of the reasons I like spelt is because of how easy it is to swap it in for all-purpose in many baking recipes.

GEOGRAPHICAL ORIGIN & ERA OF EMERGENCE: Turkey, Iran, later Central Europe, around 5000 BCE

HISTORICAL IMPORTANCE: Some culinary historians argue that bread wheats evolved from spelt (*Triticum spelta*) in the area around the Caspian Sea. It was abundant thousands of years ago, as its stability for storage and cool climates, as well as its requiring less fertilizer than many wheats, made it desirable. It is still grown today, but in much smaller quantities, and mostly by organic farmers for the same reasons that made it popular in the past.

FLAVOUR: toasty-nutty, mellow caramel, honey notes.

SPECIAL FEATURES: Spelt is an ancient wheat that is high in protein, likely derived from a hybrid of emmer wheat and emerging bread wheats; often digests better for people with wheat and gluten sensitivities.

CHALLENGES: Lacks dough elasticity for bread making during gluten development; though workable to hand knead, spelt sourdoughs benefit from frequent folder periods throughout the bulk fermentation, rather than one concentrated kneading session up front.

BEST USES: For pastries and in recipes where some properties of common wheat are desired, like gluten development. If you're making a cake

Clockwise: sprouted spelt kernels, spelt flakes, and whole spelt flour

that has a significant rise and you want to try a whole spelt flour version, you can sift out some of the larger bran particles. This also serves to aerate the flour, a good step to take for most cake recipes.

TRIVIA: Spelt was an important staple in ancient Greek and Roman societies. Though it has diminished in dietary significance in Europe, you can still find it popping up in certain recipes and grocery stores, often in its unmilled form as kernels.

Spelt Plum Crumble Squares

Makes 12–16 squares

Equipment

9 × 13–inch roasting pan

box grater or pastry blender

whisk

dough scraper, or flat-edged
    hard cooking tool (like a
    flipper or spatula)

Ingredients

7–9 medium-large dark plums,
    such as damson, zwetschgen,
    Stanley, or Italian, roughly 700 g

Dry ingredients

200 g / 1 cup sugar

1 tsp baking powder

375 g / 3 cups whole spelt flour

½ tsp cinnamon

¼ tsp nutmeg

¼ tsp salt

227 g / 1 cup cold butter

1 egg

Before heading home from Germany, I loaded my bag up with cookbooks—the only kind of German books I could understand. As I got more into whole-grain baking, I started modifying recipes, including this pflaumenkuchen, or plum cake recipe. In Germany this recipe is part of the pantheon of kuchen, or cake, though to North Americans, it is closer to what we would call a square or slab cake.

The tartness of the plums in this recipe is nicely balanced by the sweet, nutty, and spiced crumble dough. Other fruits can work, but note that plums contain less liquid than other fruits, and juicier fruits will impact the finished bake due to their respective moisture content. As such, cooking time will likely be extended if made with a juicier fruit. These squares are best served with a dollop of whipped cream on top.

Don't worry about peeling the plums. It's not only beautiful, but tempers the sweetness of the finished product with the tannins in the skin.

1. Preheat the oven to 190°C / 375°F. Grease a 9 × 13–inch roasting pan or line with parchment paper.

2. Prepare the plums by scoring them all the way down to the pit with a knife in at least 6 sections. Continue by pulling the slices off the pit. Gather in a bowl and set aside.

3. Mix all of the dry ingredients together in a medium-large bowl, using a whisk to make sure everything is well integrated.

4. Using the largest holes on a box grater, grate the cold butter onto a cutting board or directly in the bowl. Use your hands to blend the dry mix with the butter, thoroughly distributing it through the flour mix. If using a pastry cutter, cut the butter into centimetre-ish cubes with a knife. Mix into dry ingredients and use the pastry tool to cut the butter into the flour, until the pieces of butter are all a little smaller than a pea.

5. In a separate small bowl, whisk the egg with a fork. Make a well in the middle of the buttery-flour mix, and pour the egg into the centre of the well. Mix it swiftly and thoroughly into the flour and butter with a spatula until the dough starts to come together. You'll know it's ready when it forms loose crumbs that are a bit wet and the dough comes together when squeezed in your hand.

6. With wet hands, scatter about 80% of the dough (4 cups-ish) over the bottom of your prepared pan. Press the dough into a thin layer that is as uniformly thick as you can make it. If there are gaps or divets, you can take a little bit of the leftover dough and fill them in by pressing a tiny bit of dough on top.

7. Fan out the plum slices, either overlapping them slightly if they are thinner or butting them tight against one another if they are thicker. Grab small amounts of the remaining crumble dough, and scatter on top.

8. Bake at 205°C / 375°F in the lower-middle part of the oven for 40 minutes or until the crumble has slightly browned. You can tell it's done when the fruit is visibly cooked and the crumble has a deeper golden hue. Let cool for 1 hour to be able to easily lift out squares. Will keep for up to 1 week, refrigerated and sealed.

GRAIN VARIATIONS: This recipe is straightforward and will work with any whole-grain flour, such as Kamut, whole wheat, or even more assertive grains like buckwheat. The texture and flavour will shift if you switch out the spelt for another whole-grain flour, but that's the beauty of desserts like this: using a simple recipe as a base to understand how whole grains behave.

VARIATIONS

To make a smaller batch of squares, you can halve the recipe and bake it in an 8 × 8–inch square brownie pan.

This dessert can be made ahead of time by simply freezing the loose crumble and thawing it prior to pressing it into the pan.

Whole Grain Pie Pastry

Makes enough dough for 2 large pies

Pie pastry can feel hard to crack if you've never attempted it before, and even if you have, sometimes you feel like you didn't get it right. There are some important principles to making a flaky, delicious crust for your various pies (and tarts, pinwheels, and quiches, etc.). Each of these principles is built into this recipe.

The colder the better: It's important to keep your ingredients cold, especially whichever fat you are using. The colder your ingredients, the flakier your dough will be. Cold ingredients help prevent the fats from melding fully into the flour, and even protect the flecks of butter to ensure that as your pastry bakes, it becomes flaky. Do your best to handle the dough as little as possible, in part to keep the temperature of your dough low. A good tip is to chill the dough once you have rolled it into the pan but before filling, to ensure the dough is cold when it enters the oven.

Water: Pie dough can take different amounts of water to reach similar results, depending on various factors such as the way you handle the dough, the type of flour being used, even the weather or ambient temperature in the room. Whole-grain pie doughs tend to be a bit thirstier than all-purpose flour ones, but just a little. Less is more is a general rule of thumb when it comes to water.

If you're not used to working with pie dough, starting out with a blend of white and whole-grain flours can be helpful for learning to handle and bake flaky and flavourful pie pastry. But once you get the hang of it, whole-grain pie doughs will soon become your mainstay. The unique flavours and textural contributions whole-grain flours offer in pie pastry make for exciting pairings with different fruits and fillings.

Pie pastry is very versatile and can be used to host fruits or savoury fillings. Pie dough freezes well, and it feels good to have some frozen pie dough disks on hand for whenever fresh fruits or other pie pastry needs emerge.

Use this pastry for to make Spelt Date Pinwheels (see page 93) and Wild Blueberry Pie (see page 165).

1. Place cold butter in the freezer for 30 minutes to 1 hour prior to making the crust. If your kitchen is quite warm, ensure you have cold water to work with as well.

2. Grate the cold butter using the largest holes on a cheese grater. Add the butter to the bowl of flour. With a fork, mix in the cold grated butter. Here the action is swiftly and gently tossing the ingredients, not pressing.

   If using a pastry blender: cut butter into centimetre-ish cubes. Mix into dry ingredients and use the pastry blender to cut the butter into pieces that are smaller than a pea.

continued...

Equipment
box grater or pastry blender

Ingredients
650g / 5⅓ cup whole spelt flour
   OR 180g / 2⅓ cups whole
   spelt flour *plus* 360 g / 3 cups
   all-purpose flour
454 g / 2 cups salted butter*
(Add ½ tsp salt if using unsalted)
15 ml / 1 Tbsp vinegar (apple cider
   is great here)
420 ml / 1¾ cup cold water
   (depending on the flour, you
   may need a bit more or a
   bit less)

Jess grates the cold butter, integrating it into flour as needed.

Jess slowly adds cold water, distributing it evenly with a fork.

Checking to see if the dough needs any more water / holds together when clumped.

As the dough is still a bit loose, Jess compresses the chunks of dough by hand to make them stick.

Jess starts to roll out a pre-shaped, floured disk of dough.

Jess carefully places the rolled out pastry in a pie dish.

3. Mix the vinegar into the cold water. Then, carefully drizzle about ½ the water mix overtop of your butter/flour mix. Using a fork, mix until the water is evenly distributed into butter-flour mix. Now start slowly pouring the rest of the water onto your mix, stirring the dough with a fork as you pour, and mix well. Once all of the water has been incorporated into the dough, press the dough together gently until you can form a ball. You'll know you have enough water when the dough becomes sticky enough to form big clumps when squeezed with your hand.

Press the dough together gently until you can form a ball. If you can't form a ball, add a touch more water, 1 tsp or less at a time.

4. Divide the dough into 4 pieces and shape into balls. Remember: the bottom crust will use roughly 60% of the half recipe and the top disk will be the other 40%. Press the balls down, one at a time on a gently floured surface, to shape into approximately 6-inch-wide disks. You want a uniform circle before you begin rolling. So use your hands to smooth the tall edges of the disk, or roll the thick disks around gently on their sides. This will help prevent your dough from cracking when you roll it out later on.

5. Wrap each disk of dough in parchment paper and place in an airtight container. (At this stage, you can freeze the dough disks for future pie pastry creations.) Chill the dough for at least 30 minutes before rolling.

*NOTE: This recipe asks for butter, which imparts a richness of flavour but can be trickier for novice bakers, especially if you're working in a warm kitchen; it must be very cold when worked with. Butter also creates steam (butter is roughly 20% water) when it hits the oven, yielding in a flakier pastry.

When deciding which fat to use in your pastry, the considerations mainly come down to texture and flavour. I've made this recipe at home using a blend of butter and shortening, or all shortening. Shortening and lard are both neutral in flavour and tend to yield more tender crusts than butter, in part because they have a higher melting point. Both of these fats also have a longer shelf life, both in the pantry and in the finished result. Blending butter with another more neutral fat can give you the best of both worlds.

After dough has been gently pressed in the pie dish, the berry mix is added.

After trimming the overhang of dough, Jess pinches two layers of dough together.

Spelt Date Pinwheels

Makes approx. 48 pinwheels

There is a tradition of making baked goods with scrap pie crust, the leftover ends that get trimmed off. It is an exercise in thrift and indulgence, all at the same time. These little scraps are often rolled up into small pinwheels, dusted with sugar or jammed with fruit. One of the best names for these wonderful treats can be found amongst French Canadians, who are known to fill them with cinnamon and sugar, and call them pets de sœur. Nun's farts.

At my farmers' market table, these Spelt Date Pinwheels were an inexpensive two-bite treat, sold for just a dollar. They make a perfect naturally sweet, high-energy snack that packs well and is great for hikes. This particular filling strikes a balance of savoury and sweet, with the addition of coriander and cumin.

This recipe yields three logs of pinwheels that can be frozen for up to 4 months, ready to be sliced and baked off as needed. A fruit jam instead of honey can be used to bring in a fruity rather than floral flavour element. This recipe has more than one multi-hour waiting period, so read through the steps and plan accordingly.

continued...

Equipment

rolling pin

food processor or
  powerful blender

dough scraper

Ingredients

400 g pitted dates (2⅓ cups,
  compressed)

150 ml / ½ cup + Tbsp boiling
  water

½ tsp ground ginger

½ tsp ground coriander

½ tsp ground cumin

½ tsp cinnamon

½ tsp nutmeg

15 ml / 1 Tbsp honey

½ *Whole Grain Pie Pastry* (cold
  and ready to be rolled)

dusting flour for your rolling
  surface

1. Pour 150 ml boiling water over the 400 g dates in a bowl, making sure that the dates are well submerged in the hot water. Leave to sit for at least 4 hours.

2. Puree the soaked dates along with the spices in a food processor until smooth. Allow the date mixture to cool to room temperature, or place in the fridge until you're ready to use. If the filling is warm or hot, it will melt the fat and make for a tougher pastry.

3. Flour your work surface, and both sides of your dough. Take the dough and shape it into a small rectangle. To achieve this dimension, you will be mostly rolling the dough lengthwise.

   If your pastry is round, you can make corners by using the palm of your hand to press outwards at equally distant points around the disk.

4. You're looking to roll the dough until it is roughly 9 × 30 inches. To extend the corners of your dough sheet out, roll diagonally, straight into the corners of the dough.

   Sometimes the rolling pin gets sticky with dough and wiping it clean with a bit of flour can be useful. Dust the top of your work surface and check occasionally that the bottom isn't stuck by trying to slide it. If it is stuck, carefully free the dough from below with a scraper or flat spatula and slide it gently out of your rolling zone. These steps will fully reset your station so you can keep rolling the dough to the desired size.

5. When you have reached the right size, take a knife and trim the edges of the dough sheet so that it is a close to perfect rectangle. You can use the trim to patch thin spots or create a straight side on one of the rougher edges.

6. Take the cooled date filling and evenly spread it over the whole sheet, getting it as level as you can. You can use a dough scraper or another flat-edged tool for this.

7. Cut the pastry into 3 equal quadrants measuring 9 x 10 inches and roll each one up into a log, rolling the 10-inch side up. Roll tightly so that there are no air pockets, but not so tightly that you squeeze the filling out.

8. Place the rolls in the freezer until the dough feels firm enough that it doesn't dent easily when you poke it, at least 2 hours or overnight. (If leaving overnight, make sure to wrap the rolls in clingfilm.) They need to be frozen enough so that when you slice them, they won't be squished or deformed, but not so hard that you crack the pastry when sliced. If the logs are fully frozen, let them warm up slightly for about 1 hour (as long as your kitchen is not too hot) before slicing.

9. Preheat oven to 190°C / 375°F.

10. With a very sharp or serrated knife, slice each log into pinwheels roughly 1 cm thick. Space out on a cookie sheet with about 1 inch in between each pinwheel. If the wheels are getting flattened as you cut, try refreezing them until they are a bit firmer, or rotate the wheel so you aren't always putting the knife pressure at the same point on the log.

11. Bake pinwheels for 20 minutes and then remove from the oven and flip them over. Finish by baking for another 10 minutes or until the pastry is golden and the date mixture look caramelized.
    Transfer to a cooling rack, and let cool on the pan.

Linzer Torte

Makes 1 torte

When it comes to nuts, almonds versus hazelnuts is a long-standing debate in my mind. But hazelnuts almost always come out on top because of my love for their distinct and prominent flavour. I find them woodsy in character, not in a resinous or piney way, but tannic and slightly bitter, like good dark chocolate. I often leave the skins on, because for better or for worse, part of my baking philosophy is taking the path of least resistance. If skins are going to add some flavour complexity as well as fibre and nutrients, why add the work to remove?

I went hard for hazelnut-based foods while living in Germany, including many different kinds of cakes and chocolates. To me, Linzer torte, a traditional German dessert that originated in Austria, is a rich show-stopper worth knowing and making. It is luxurious from the fat of the nuts, which play well with spelt, as well as the warmth of the spices. After much experimentation, I landed on a mix of hazelnuts and almonds for my personal Linzer torte. Almonds mellow out the intensity of the hazelnuts and bring a creaminess to the texture of the final baked good, despite its coarse crumb. Using only almonds or hazelnuts is also an option if that suits you best.

This torte can be assembled and refrigerated for 24 hours or assembled and frozen ahead of time and thawed, with an egg wash to finish it just prior to baking. You can create a lattice for the top or use cookie cutter shapes to create a pattern.

continued...

Equipment

food processor

whisk

box grater

rolling pin (wine bottle works in
a pinch)

cookie cutter

10-inch springform pan
(a 9 × 9–inch square pan will
also work)

pastry brush

Ingredients

180 g / 1½ cup whole almonds
and/or hazelnuts*

270 g / 2 cups whole spelt flour

150 g / ½ cup + 3 Tbsp white or
cane sugar

1 tsp ground cinnamon

½ tsp ground nutmeg

1 tsp baking powder

150 g / ⅔ cup cold butter

2 eggs (1 whole and 1 separated)

30 ml / 2 Tbsp rum (or other
aromatic booze)

250ml raspberry jam (though you
could substitute other fruit
jams or fruit butters)

dusting flour for rolling surface

* A NOTE ON NUTS: Freshly
ground makes a difference in the
taste and texture of this recipe,
but it will still be delicious with
pre-ground nuts. Just make sure
to taste your nuts ahead of time
to make sure they're still good.
Rancid nuts can ruin a dish.

1. Place all the nuts in a food processor with ⅓ of the total flour in the recipe (about ⅔ cup spelt flour). Grind in a food processor until you can see the nuts getting fairly fine as they blend into the flour. This step allows the flour to absorb some of the oil coming off the nuts and prevents the nuts from clumping as they are ground.

2. Crack one into a small bowl and then separate the second egg, setting the yolk aside and adding the whites to the existing whole egg. (It will be used at the end in a glaze for the unbaked torte)

3. Using a whisk, mix all the dry ingredients—the remaining flour, sugar, spices, baking powder, and the ground nut-flour mix. Make sure everything is well combined.

4. Using a cheese grater, grate the cold butter straight into the dry-mix bowl or onto a plate. After it's grated, using a fork or your hands—break up all of the butter shreds, making a dry dough that is flecked with butter. Once evenly distributed, make a well in the centre of the dry mix.

5. Mix the eggs with the rum and stir into the well and onto the shaggy dry mix. Using a fork, spatula, or hands, swiftly mix the wet and dry together until you get big, coarse wet crumbs.

6. Line your springform pan with parchment paper.

7. Measure off 190 g (approximately 1⅓ cups) of this dough and set aside to save for rolling the top. Press the remainder of the shaggy dough into the parchment-lined springform pan. Using a dough scraper or the flat side of a metal spatula, press down the crumb mix. By the end of this step, there should be no loose dough bits. Go along the edges, pressing down to make it as even and level as possible.

8. Pour jam overtop the pressed dough. Use the flat-edged tool you used in the previous stage to level the jam in an even layer on top of the dough.

9. At this point, start preheating your oven to 175°C / 350°F.

Whisking the wet ingredients together in well.

Pressing the linzer dough into the pan as evenly as possible.

Pouring jam over the pressed dough.

10. Dust a flat work surface with flour. Take your remaining dough and knead a tablespoonful of flour into it and then into a ball. Flatten this into a disk and then roll out with a rolling pin. Every few rolls with the pin, re-dust the top of the disk and make sure you can still slide the disk around without it sticking. Flour your rolling pin as well.

If dough is sticking on the bottom, free it with a flat-edged tool and slide it around so it can grab the residual dusting flour underneath.

11. Use cookie cutters to lay a unique design over the jam layer. Take your cookie cutter or ring and dip it in your dusting flour pile.

Alternatively, you could do lattice work. Roll out the top dough so that inch-wide strips will span the width of the springform pan. Cut the dough into strips using a knife or a tool with a crinkle edge if available. Make sure your disk is wide enough that the strips will span the different widths of the springform pan from side to side, and in the other direction across.

Carefully laying the yolk-washed Linzer shapes.

12. Before laying the strips or shapes, whisk the yolk with 1 teaspoon of water. Brush the strips with the yolk mix using a pastry brush. Lay the strips in a lattice pattern, gently trimming the lengths with a knife where they meet the edge of the pan.

13. Bake at 350°F for 1 hour.

14. Allow to cool completely before cutting.

VARIATIONS

You can take any excess top dough and reroll to complete the design or cut into shapes for Linzer cookies. If you bake any leftovers in cookie form, brush with yolk mix and bake for 12 minutes at 350°F / 175°C.

KAMUT/ KHORASAN
(Triticum turgidum)

Kamut/Khorasan is an interesting variety of wheat for many reasons. Firstly, because of its dual name, with Kamut being a commercial trademark for the grain while Khorasan refers to the region in Central Asia that encompasses parts of northern Iran and Afghanistan, where the grain is thought to have originated. Most Kamut/Khorasan wheat is grown in North America and is also a grain crop in parts of the Mediterranean, Turkey, North Africa, Kazakhstan, and Iran.

GEOGRAPHICAL ORIGIN & ERA OF EMERGENCE: Before it was known as Kamut, Khorasan wheat emerged close to 10,000 years ago in what is often called the Fertile Crescent, encompassing Iraq, Syria, Lebanon, Jordan, pre-1948 Palestine, Cyprus, Southeastern Turkey, and Western Iran. This area is considered the cradle of wheat, where many grains and cereals originated, anchoring themselves in human society. Ancient wheats and other early grain crops allowed humans to stay in place for more of the year,

moving away from nomadic forms of agriculture. It is an ancient relative of durum wheat (*Triticum durum*), a high-protein (high-gluten) wheat.

HISTORICAL IMPORTANCE: Khorasan would have been an important grain in the cuisine and culture of Egyptian society during the time of the pharaohs, used for beer and bread. It was popularized by the father-son duo of Mack and Bob Quinn, who went on to trademark the name of Kamut for the grain. This grain may have a modern name, but it gives us culinary insight into what the landscape of cultivated wheats would have been like 3,000 years ago.

FLAVOUR: buttery, velvety, sweet nuttiness, earthy.

SPECIAL FEATURES: Kamut protein percentages (i.e. gluten) are higher than bread wheats, though the gluten strands aren't as strong as those of wheat gluten. By acre, Kamut has a lower yield than common wheats, though its kernel size is almost twice the weight of bread wheats. With higher protein (gluten), Kamut contains more amino acids for digestibility. It can withstand drier growing conditions than many wheat

Kamut kernels (left) and whole Khorasan flour (right).

varieties, though it is more disease prone, especially if there is a wet harvest season.

CHALLENGES: Khorasan behaves like wheat in many ways, though it is more closely related to a pasta wheat than a bread wheat, meaning it absorbs water differently. When working with whole grain Kamut flours, start with a little less water or liquid in your doughs, and add slowly as you mix. You may also need more than your recipe requests. Sifted or white Kamut flour performs impeccably close to all-purpose wheat flour.

BEST USES: Sourdough bread, pancakes and other skillet cakes; denser cakes. Like many whole grains, Khorasan has a wonderful nuttiness that pairs well with seeds like pumpkin or sesame. It also has a butteriness to it, and even a sweet resemblance to corn. Even if it is often considered an ancient grain or ancient wheat, truly, it behaves like modern wheats, and is a great choice for making a lofty, yet hefty whole grain bread.

TRIVIA: The story of how Khorasan came to be known as Kamut can be traced back to 1944, when a US soldier was given 36 Khorasan wheat kernels in Portugal. He passed them on to his father, a farmer in Montana. Over the coming decades, the grain became popular amongst farmers in that region of the American midwest. By the 1960s its origin story had morphed into a myth about a Montana farm boy who stumbled upon thirty-six kernels inside a tomb in Egypt, who later sowed them with his father at home. Around this time, Khorasan wheat became locally named "King Tut's Wheat."

When attempting to brand this special grain seed, a different farmer found the word *Kamut* in the only Egyptology book at a small library in Montana. It suggested that *Kamut* was an ancient word meaning "wheat." Two prairie business-minded farmers, Mack and Bob Quinn, believed in Kamut as a crop, and in 1989 Kamut was trademarked, with a requirement for farmers to follow organic growing methods in its commercial production.

The company Kamut International Ltd. heavily marketed this product, arguably resulting in any familiarity you likely have with it. In a sense, Kamut is a species that is privately owned by North Americans, with its production and processing concentrated in Montana in the US and Alberta and Saskatchewan in Canada. This seed project and company is unique (because of its organic legislation), though also problematic and appropriative. Kamut LTD was attempting to address shortcomings of the commodity grain industry by requiring that any food called Kamut be certified organically grown. The company also assures that farmers get a guaranteed price, unlike the commodity wheat market. They also buy back Kamut harvests from the farmers they sell seed to and process and distribute specially milled Kamut flour.

Along the Way

Before I could confidently bake with whole grains, I had many teachers who took me under their wing.

Throughout my years of running bread subscriptions and selling my wares at farmers' markets, I continued to hone my craft by visiting other bakers and their respective bakeries. I was still renting a space to bake out of, constantly wondering if and how I might one day have a custom bakery space. A poet friend and I decided to set off on a 20,000-kilometre road trip across the US and back. We were both seeking out our teachers. For my friend Ben, it was poets he appreciated. For me, it was the bakers I had met through The Kneading Conference, and the wider network of grain obsessives they'd connected me to.

Bakers are something of a unique breed. Often falling into a few archetypes, they tend to be artistic engineers, sensitive thinkers, ambitious planners, and industrious and calculating workers. They also occasionally are beholden by systematic yet chaotic dispositions. This accurately sums up my disposition: a philosopher-chemist-type baker, holding the symbol, power, and cultural meaning of bread close to me as I worked out fermentation formulas and schedules.

Getting to know old-world methods for bread making also meant learning about the legacy of bread to society, and learning about alternative grains revealed the long relationship and old science of growing, milling, and crafting breads. The whole-grain and wood-fired bakers I was connecting with were all unique alchemists, making meaningful magic happen day in and day out.

Despite having started a bakery so quickly, my commitment to baking was slow in the making (I'm a libra, what can I say). Throughout that two-month drive, I saw many different wood-fired ovens, bakeries, and so much more, sometimes getting to bake alongside thoughtful, talented teachers. I witnessed the brilliance of bakers from state to state, and I was enthralled and comforted by resonating so strongly with them, their practices, their ideas. These bakers pushed me past the point of no return. In a way, I had found my people.

After surviving an epic flu that lasted from Sante Fe to Los Angeles, Ben and I headed to our ultimate destination of Cohasset, California, just north of Sacramento. This is where we would visit Roger Jansen, a legendary flour mill and oven builder. We had met two years prior at The Kneading Conference. Roger, his son Larry (the baker), daughter-in-law Chris (the problem solver), and Vann (the baker's cool kid) all ran a majestic whole-grain, wood-fired-oven sourdough bakery called Hearth and Stone. It was a hideaway in the woods nestled in the foothills of the Sierra Nevada mountains.

Their creative compound featured Chris and Larry's house, Roger's cabin, the bakery, a workshop for building flour mills, the woodshed, along with a pottery studio and storage shed for Roger's ceramic creations. Outside were bread ovens being developed here and there. Ben and I stayed for a full week and immersed ourselves in their routine, enjoying the pace of their home-bakery workweek, learning about milling history from Roger, while Ben cooked lots of impressive dinners for us as we got to know our new friends.

The Jansens taught me a lot about bread, milling, and baking that week. I saw how rewarding and multifaceted a passion for bread can be: the pleasure and practice of it, what it can mean to buy grain directly from a farmer (socially, economically, agriculturally) and to have dialogue with these grain growers. I learned how to literally listen to the grain itself while it's being milled, tuning in to the uniqueness of different grains, to find out how to best mill and bake them.

Larry, like other whole grain lovers, had come to embrace the trial and error involved in commercial whole-grain baking, not to mention all that comes with whole-grain sourdough baking. The bakes were daily experiments with different parameters, controls, and variables. I took notice of the records Larry would keep—recording many different temperatures, the timing of specific steps, the weather, humidity, and the mood. Larry and Roger, the baker-miller-engineer duo extraordinaire, showed me that baking was a way to manifest the scientist I imagined myself growing up to become. And that all results are valid.

Did I mention that bread made with custom-milled flour, baked in a wood-fired oven is otherworldly delicious? At Hearth and Stone, the workweek began with the ritual of milling flour for the upcoming bakes. Stone mills are designed so the miller can fine-tune the grind, learning to correlate the sound the grain makes as it passes through the mill stones with the different possible textures of flour being ground. With an ear to the literal grindstone, eventually followed by the ability to let it run, stone mills can be calibrated so the baker can multitask while the mill does its thing. I was starting to see more clearly how fundamental milling is to how whole-grain breads turn out, regardless of whether or not it is sourdough.

At Hearth and Stone, Larry was the main baker, but Chris was logistics manager and assistant baker. Roger was the engineer and welder, though he and Larry built their mills together. Larry and I spent a few days working in the bakery. He showed me the way he made whole-grain sourdoughs, starting with his desem-style wheat starter, which he called Mom. We worked on a rye starter together as he was unfamiliar with rye sourdoughs. I was able to share my formula and tricks for a 100% rye bread, a recipe he integrated into his own bakery lineup.

I got to touch, taste, and smell the different textures and hydrations of his whole-grain flour sourdough formulas. Some things were similar and some things were different from the recipes I had been cultivating the two years I had been

Portrait of a baker, 2016.

a baker. The breads from Larry's bakery were varied, unique, and incredibly delicious. After having yet again encountered wood-fired ovens, having one became a priority for my own future dream bakery. And when I had one, I would start making a version of his sesame whole wheat bread almost immediately.

Larry was the first baker I saw working with an ancient grain that had always intrigued me, but hadn't encountered in Germany: Kamut, also called Khorasan wheat. It had such a unique feel in my hand, a fine particulate but not as soft as other wheat flours. Larry had it perfectly milled. We baked bread and pastries with it, and I got to witness its unique texture change from preparation to preparation. Depending on the hydration (from water or milk) or the richness of the dough (from fats), I watched it react and become silky as it merged with eggs and butter. Working with this golden grain and

seeing how it can be softened and worked into a gorgeous, delicate, yet glutinous and springy dough is cause for celebration and devotion to the whole-grain revolution.

Over the course of the week, I witnessed various grains in the bakery go from whole dried seed to flour, to sourdough sponge, to final dough, to a fermented and proofed raw loaf, ready to hit the floor of a hot oven that had been firing and storing heat in its stones. There is nothing quite like watching a hearth loaf, placed into a 700°F oven, springing up and out in response to hitting the hot fire brick. Baking is fundamentally scientific in that you are working with different forms of chemical reactions, be they baking soda and heat in a cake or fermenting flour in a sourdough. Throw in sticks, stones, and flames, and you've got yourself a pretty cool lab.

Kamut Walnut Tea Ring

Makes 2 rings

Traditionally, tea rings are great as a lightly sweet snack for tea time. This recipe comes from one of my whole-grain sourdough mentors, Larry Jansen. Larry is the son of Roger Jansen, who I met at The Kneading Conference in Skowhegan, Maine. It was thanks to him, during a visiting with Roger and Larry in Northern California, that I really fell for Kamut.

Walnut tea rings smell incredible fresh from the oven, as the brown sugar caramel enrobing the raisins and walnuts bubbles out to create a perfect sugar crisp for the baker to snack on once it cools. When I make this recipe, I like to share one ring with a friend and keep one—eating at least a third of it right away, and then slowly cutting off sections and savouring this snack as it disappears over the days to come.

This recipe is an enriched dough, meaning butter and eggs are involved. They are key to a brioche dough, adding a richness to this sourdough sweet bread. Also, try and push how long you can go before re-dusting your surface and hands, as you don't want to incorporate more flour than is actually required. This is the part of whole-grain bread making that comes with practice, and yields so much satisfaction.

continued...

Equipment
pastry brush
rolling pin
scissors
parchment paper

Ingredients
Sourdough Sponge
20 g / 1 Tbsp starter
70 g / ½ cup whole Kamut flour
50 ml water

Final Dough
50 g / ¼ cup sugar
1 egg
76 g / ⅓ cup butter
95 ml milk
285 g / 1¾ cup whole Kamut flour
7g / 1 tsp salt
dusting flour for work surface

Filling
75 g / ½ cup raisins
55g / ½ cup roughly chopped
   walnuts
80g / ½ cup packed brown sugar
   (regular sugar or cane sugar
   will work too)
1½ tsp cinnamon
½ tsp nutmeg

Finish
1 egg, mixed well with a fork for
   an egg wash

1. Mix the ingredients for your Sourdough Sponge together the night before you want to make the rings. Let the sponge mix stand overnight or 8–14 hours. (Remember to refresh your starter at least 12 hours and up 3 days before mixing the sponge ingredients.)

2. The next morning, or when the sponge is ripe (look for signs it has bubbled and grown, but not collapsed), add the sponge to a bowl and mix with the sugar, egg, butter, milk, Kamut flour, and salt from the Final Dough ingredients. Knead in a bowl for a minute or two until it all comes together, then let it rest for a 30–45 minute autolyse.

3. Come back to the dough and turn it out onto a flat surface and knead it for 5–7 minutes. Dust your work surface and hands with flour as needed to be able to keep the dough from sticking to the surface and your hands. When your hands and surface are freshly floured, it will stick the least.

4. Next, let the dough rest for a 2-hour-long bulk fermentation. Once complete, degas the dough by kneading it for about 30 seconds. Then let the dough sit for 30–45 minutes.

5. While the dough sits, soak the walnuts and raisins in hot water for five minutes and then strain. Leave this mix to drip dry in a strainer for the 30 to 45 minutes while your dough is resting. After they have strained, take the raisin-and-walnut mixture, and mix in a small bowl with the sugar, nutmeg, and cinnamon. Set aside.

6. Degas the dough by punching it down one final time and split into 2 pieces. Shape the first piece into a small, narrow log shape. Dust your work surface and roll out the dough lengthwise on a smooth flat surface until it is 16 inches long and no narrower than 5 inches wide.

continued...

Kamut Walnut Tea Ring filling mixture.

Preparing Kamut Walnut Tea Ring.

Snipping short cuts in egg-washed Kamut Walnut Tea Rings just before baking.

7. Turn the dough so the length of it is running parallel to the front of your body. Carefully distribute half of the raisin mix along the centre of your dough strip, from end to end. It should be about ¾ cup or 125 g. Once the mix is all spread out, close up the roll by wrapping the exposed dough up and around the length of the strip, tucking the walnut raisin mix fully inside. Pinch the dough where it overlaps on itself. Once sealed, form the ring by taking the two ends and blending them together. Overlap and then pinch the two ends together. You can use your hands to blend the seams a bit.

8. Repeat for the second ring and move the rings, with the seal on the underside, onto a cookie sheet lined with parchment paper. Your rings should be about 7 inches in diameter. Let the rings rest for 30 minutes.

9. Preheat your oven to 205°C / 400°F during this final proof.

10. Just prior to baking, brush the rings with your egg wash. Take kitchen shears/scissors and snip short cuts in the top of the ring, no longer than 1 inch each. There should be about 8 to 10 snips, placed evenly around the ring.

11. Bake at 400°F / 205°C for approximately 25 minutes. Tea rings are delicious served warm or at room temperature. Store for up to 5 days.

Kinako Kamut Cookies

Makes about 3-dozen cookies

For my thirtieth birthday, I treated myself to a trip to Japan. For five weeks I ate and adventured around on my own, making friends along the way. Eating in Japan forever changed the way I think about food, expanding my understanding of grain-based cuisines. Encountering the wonder of kinako was one such lesson.

I've loved soy ever since my short-lived vegan era in the mid-2000s. Alas, soy is a food often villainized within wellness culture (just like flour), but I will always defend its honour. Soy is a beloved Japanese legume and kinako is one of its forms, made from ground and roasted soybeans. Processing soy this way brings out malty caramel notes. One of the first ways I tried kinako was a seasoning for mochi cakes toasted on a hibachi.

I brought home a package of kinako from Japan and merged it with Kamut to make this cookie recipe at a local craft fair I used to vend at twice a year. Kinako and Kamut together are well matched, their flavours and textures boosted by the specks of crunchy pumpkin seeds that roast on the edges of the cookies as they bake. Kinako flour can be sourced from health-food and international grocery stores.

continued...

Equipment
electric mixer or whisk

Ingredients
75 g / ⅔ cup kinako flour
215 g / 1½ cups whole Kamut flour
1 tsp baking powder
75 g / ½ cup pumpkin seeds
170 g / ¾ cup butter,
    room temperature
154 g / ¾ cup sugar (cane or
    brown sugar is best but white
    will work too)
1 egg
½ tsp vanilla

Kamut and kinako flours side by side before mixing.

1. Combine the Kamut and kinako flours and baking powder together. Whisk or sift to remove lumps and aerate the dry ingredients. To prepare for a later step, finely chop ⅓ cup of pumpkin seeds and set aside.

2. Mix butter and the sugar together for 3 minutes vigorously with a whisk or with a mixer. Add the egg and mix for another minute. Add vanilla and whisk until thoroughly combined.

3. Add the flour mix to the batter, and mix until the dough is homogenous. (If it is looking sandy or dry, don't worry, keep mixing until you can see that everything is thoroughly blended). Finish the dough by kneading gently by hand for up to 1 minute.

4. Divide the dough into 2 even pieces. Roll each dough chunk into a log approximately 6 inches long and 1½ tall. You can roll this shorter and fatter if you would like to make fewer, larger cookies.
    If you find the dough to be too sticky, rolling the logs while the dough is wrapped in parchment paper is a nice technique. If cracks appear in your logs, you can try kneading a bit more or smoothing them over by massaging the crack with your fingers.

Slicing Kinako Kamut Cookie log.

5. To finish the logs, scatter the chopped pumpkin seeds on a plate and roll the logs around on top, pressing the dough and seeds as needed to get them to stick. Any excess can be gently pressed onto the logs by hand, patching any gaps.

6. Refrigerate the logs for at least 1 hour. You want the logs to be so firm that when you go to slice them with a sharp knife, the pressure of the knife doesn't misshape or flatten your log. You can also freeze the logs (or just one) to thaw, slice, and bake at a later date.

7. Preheat the oven to 175°C / 350°F.

8. Slice each log into approximately 18 round cookies. Each cookie should be about 5–8 mm. If the cookie logs start to flatten on the bottom as you slice, try throwing the logs into the freezer for a few minutes or rotating the log a quarter turn every couple of slices.

9. Place cookies on two baking sheets and bake one at a time at 175 °C / 350°F for about 13–15 minutes or until the cookies are golden brown.

10. Let cool completely for a few hours before storing in an airtight container for up to 1 week.

Kamut, Carrot, Apple & Pumpkin Seed Salad

Makes 8–10 servings

Many of the grains in this book can and are often cooked whole as kernels, similar to the way you would cook rice. Though it's rare for most cereal grains to become as creamy as rice, grains are often cooked as part of a meal no matter where in the world they grow, served either hot or cold, and often in salads like this one. You can quite easily swap out the Kamut kernels in this recipe for another hearty whole cereal grain, such as farro or barley. I recommend soaking the Kamut kernels for a few hours ahead of time to soften them prior to cooking.

This salad is a great complement to a leafy salad.

1. In a pot, bring the Kamut kernels and water to a boil. Turn the heat down, cover the pot, and simmer the kernels for 45 minutes once they come to a boil.

2. Test by trying a kernel after 35 minutes. You'll know they are ready once the kernels have softened substantially but still retain a bit of chewiness. Take them off the heat and strain the kernels in a sieve. Return them to the pot, and cover for 15 minutes to finish softening.

3. While the kernels are softening, prepare the other ingredients. Toast the pumpkin seeds in a dry frying pan until they become fragrant, about 1 minute or so. Set aside to cool.

4. Chop apples into fairly small pieces and then toss with lemon juice in the bottom of a medium bowl. Add the grated carrots and sliced onions.

Equipment
sifter
saucepan

Ingredients
Salad
70 g / ⅓ Kamut kernels
35 g / ¼ cup toasted pumpkin
    seeds
1 medium, finely diced apple
    (tossed with 1 tsp of the lemon
    juice below once cut)
2 medium carrots, grated on the
    largest holes of the box grater
750 ml / 3 cups water, for boiling
½ tsp salt for boiling water
2 Tbsp finely sliced red onion
30 ml / 2 Tbsp lemon juice,
    roughly half a lemon
optional: 70 g / ⅓ cup feta cheese

Dressing
1 tsp chopped fresh dill
30 ml / 2 Tbsp olive oil
1 small clove garlic (grated or
    pressed)
½ tsp salt
finishing pepper
5 ml / 1 tsp cider or other fruity
    vinegar

continued...

5. Prepare the salad dressing in a jar by combining the Dressing ingredients and stir until emulsified.

6. Once the kernels have fully softened, fill the pot with cold water and let soak for a minute before straining again and letting them drip dry.

7. Once the Kamut kernels have drained and are no longer hot, add them to the other salad ingredients already in the medium bowl. Toss it all together with ¾ of the dressing until well mixed. To chill all ingredients, place covered in the fridge for at least 30 minutes and up to 24 hours.

8. To serve, toss half of the feta and pumpkin seeds with the salad. Garnish by drizzling the remaining dressing and scattering the remaining pumpkin seeds, feta, and dill.

BUCKWHEAT
(Fagopyrum esculentum)

Buckwheat is an enigmatic baking ingredient, a character unto itself. It presents itself with distinction in flavour, texture, and use, no matter the recipe. This is because the flavour is pungent, fruity, grassy, and pleasingly bitter.

For years I've been baking with Japanese buckwheat sourced from a local mill. It's a beautiful purplish shade, hued significantly by its ground-up husk in the flour mix. The colour of the flour is often a reflection of the amount of husk left in the flour, which also contains much of buckwheat's flavour and nutrients.

GEOGRAPHICAL ORIGIN & ERA OF EMERGENCE: This special edible plant evolved in a different part of the world than the rest of the cereal grains we've covered so far, originating in southwestern China and the Himalayas. Although it is often associated with Japan, where it is has been cultivated for over seven hundred years, the earliest records for cultivation are from the Balkans, and even southern Siberia.

HISTORICAL IMPORTANCE: Buckwheat can thrive in colder and higher elevation climates than most grains, which is why it thrived as a crop in mountainous east Asian regions long ago. It is eaten in various forms and dishes throughout much of Europe and Asia, from crepes in Brittany—where it is known as blé noir or sarrasin—to small savoury pancakes known as blinis throughout much of Eastern Europe.

FLAVOUR: chocolatey bitter, tangy, nutty, floral/woodsy, smoky, rich fruit-earthy. Buckwheat is a common crop grown for honey. I love pairing honey and buckwheat together (see Honey Buckwheat Brownies on page 118). Sometimes I just love matching intense aromas, leaning into their in-your-face flavour.

SPECIAL FEATURES: Buckwheat is the only grain in this book that is neither a cereal grain nor grass. It is classified as a *pseudocereal*, meaning it is used like a cereal or grain but is not botanically related to either, similar to amaranth or quinoa. Buckwheat is related to sorrel and rhubarb and its seeds are technically a tiny dried fruit. This helps explain why this grain has such a distinctive essence, both in flavour and texture.

CHALLENGES: Buckwheat flour is gluten-free, so it doesn't have binding power in baking (this is why so many soba noodles are buckwheat blended with wheat); its flavour can be very dominating, which I actually love about it. As such, it needs to be used in accordance with its characteristics rather than against them, otherwise it can overtake the flavour or texture of a baked good. One way to deal with this is to blend with a glutinous flour for some binding power and loft. Blending buckwheat 50/50 with all-purpose gives you a pretty versatile flour mix that will still be capable of a lighter-textured baked good.

Clockwise: buckwheat kernels, kasha toasted buckwheat, and stone-ground whole buckwheat flour.

BEST USES: Buckwheat is an undeniably great grain for making crepes or pancakes. You can swap in buckwheat for the Rustic Pancakes recipe on page 139. I love the flavour it gives in breads, and it blends well with other grains, like wheat and even rye.

Often when I'm tasked with gluten-free baking, I choose a recipe where I know buckwheat will be complementary, like in brownies where there is no need for the development of gluten. Baked goods that use buckwheat are often dependent on the use of a leavener, such as baking powder or whipped egg whites, to create lift, so keep that in mind if you're looking to adapt your recipes for buckwheat.

Buckwheat also really likes high-hydration/-liquid doughs or batters, as it absorbs liquid very well. Like rye, buckwheat is sometimes scalded, meaning that hot boiling water is poured over the flour. And like rye, the texture of the scalded flour is a bit more gluey or sticky.

Scalding like this benefits the final texture of certain baked goods using buckwheat. Even time can be beneficial when using buckwheat, as doughs and batters can benefit from leaving the batter or dough to sit, allowing the particles of flour to bloom and absorb all of that liquid, yielding a softer texture rather than a possibly gritty one.

Whole soaked buckwheat groats can also be great for adding to bread or muffins. If you want to have a lighter, more buttery, toasty flavour you can seek out kasha, which is roasted buckwheat groats.

TRIVIA: Buckwheat stems contain bast fibres (like hemp and flax), which are used to make fabric, twine, and rope. Buckwheat was a popular crop grown by early Acadians, especially in parts of Northern New Brunswick and Maine. In that part of Acadie, recipes for ployes—a type of buckwheat flatbread—are still made to this day.

Honey Buckwheat Brownies

Makes 12 brownies

Equipment

muffin pan

paper muffin cups (if you don't
have cups, generously grease
the muffin tin)

double boiler or equivalent
(a medium saucepan with a
bowl that covers and fits the
top of the saucepan snugly
will work well)

Ingredients

160 g / 1 cup of chopped
chocolate

150 g / ⅔ cup salted butter

3 eggs, room temperature

170 g / ½ cup honey

½ tsp vanilla (or almond extract)

75 g / ½ cup buckwheat flour

¼ tsp salt (½ tsp if using unsalted
butter)

The original name for this recipe was Independent Brownies. The recipe and the name come from one of my baking teachers, Doug Brown, who baked the brownies in muffin cups so each one comes out of the oven independent from all the rest. Baking with whole grains makes you independent too!

Buckwheat and honey are strong flavours, which helps set this brownie recipe apart from others. By the same token, the quality and variety of the chocolate used will also impact their final flavour. This recipe can be made with milk chocolate, even chocolate chips in a pinch, but buckwheat and dark chocolate are a match made in heaven.

One of the fun benefits of these brownies is that they can be suited to your personal textural preferences. If you take these out of the oven a bit early, they will be incredibly fudgey, almost like a molten chocolate cake. When baked for a little bit longer, they set a bit firmer, while still being very floral and creamy.

Straight out of the freezer or chilled is also a nice way to serve these buckwheat chocolate treats.

1. Preheat the oven to 180° C / 350°F.

2. Place a small to medium saucepan on the stove with a couple inches of water, and bring it to a boil. Once the water is boiling, place the double boiler or bowl on top of the pot. Add the butter and chocolate into the bowl or boiler.

3. Mix the butter and chocolate until completely melted and well incorporated. Set aside.

4. Whisk the eggs in a medium bowl. Add the honey and vanilla to the eggs and mix well.

5. Combine the flour and salt in a separate bowl.

6. Combine the chocolate and butter with the honey, eggs, and vanilla. Fold in the flour mix. Stir until all the flour is absorbed.

7. Pour a shy ¼ cup of batter into each muffin cup. Distribute any leftovers into the cups to even them out.

8. Bake the brownies for 25–30 minutes.

9. Remove brownies from the pan after they have cooled for 10–20 minutes. Store in an airtight container for up to 1 week.

NOTE: This is *technically* a gluten-free brownie. I say technically because to be truly gluten-free, any and all of the implements and flour you are using need to have never been in contact with any kind of gluten. Thankfully, we are starting to see more flour and grain mills with separate facilities for milling buckwheat, with mills that have never touched any gluten-bearing grains. If you can remember—and disclose—to your brownie-eating friends with gluten intolerance whether your gluten-free buckwheat has been milled at a completely gluten-free facility, you'll be golden. Thankfully, you don't have to be on a gluten-free diet to enjoy these beauties.

VARIATIONS

There are various ways of finishing these brownies, either by dusting them with a bit of high-quality cocoa or topping each brownie with an almond or two in the centre just before baking. Or, to boost the nuttiness of the finished brownie, swap the vanilla for almond extract.

Buckwheat Blueberry Grunt

Makes 6–8 servings

Blueberry grunt is a delight to say *and* to eat. Although common in much of Atlantic Canada, this dish of stewed blueberries topped with a biscuity-dumpling dough was not part of my particular New Brunswick household. I have been told that very similar dishes of dumpling-topped stewed fruit exist with their own fun names, from Bluberry Slump to Blueberry Bang Belly. Like most humble and homey dishes, they can sometimes be more than the sum of their parts. In this sweet preparation, the dumpling dough cooks and absorbs the colourful liquid, resulting in juicy, pillowy steamed biscuits nested on top of hot and sweet just-cooked blueberries.

It was when I moved to Nova Scotia, land of wild blueberries and blueberry picking, that the Grunt crossed my path. It was during a spontaneous post-beach dinner, where a good friend whipped up a blueberry grunt and blew my mind.

Other fruits will work as well, especially berries, though you may need to adjust with a touch of liquid, depending on the amount of juice your chosen fruits yield when cooked. Ice cream can be fun to serve with grunt. It provides a nice hot and cold contrast in the mouth as it melts, creating a creamy fruit sauce below.

1. Place the berries, water, and sugar in a soup pot or Dutch oven with a lid. The pot should be large enough to accommodate both the stewed fruit and the dumplings.

2. Bring to a boil and then lower the heat to simmer for a few minutes. The mixture will get quite juicy and then start to thicken a bit from the natural pectin in the fruit.

3. Meanwhile, in a medium bowl, mix the flour, baking powder, salt, and sugar. Whisk the dry mix to ensure no lumps are left in the dough, or sift the mix from one bowl into another.

4. Cut in the butter or other fat into the flour mixture with a fork or a pastry blender.

5. Once the fat is well distributed, slowly pour in the milk and mix it in with a fork as you go. The dough will just come together.

6. Remove the fruit pot from heat. Carefully drop in the dough, using two large spoons to scatter big dollops of dough gently into the hot fruit until all the batter is gone. Cover with a lid and return the pot to a low-medium heat. Set a timer for 15 minutes, and make sure to keep the lid on during this time as the dumplings are steam-cooking inside.

7. Serve Buckwheat Blueberry Grunt with a large serving spoon while hot, either on its own or with whipped cream, coconut dessert whip, or yogurt.

Equipment
soup pot or Dutch oven
pastry blender

Ingredients
Stewed fruit
750 g / 4 cups small blueberries or a mix of berries
100 g / ½ cup sugar or maple syrup
125 ml / ½ cup of water

Dumplings
65g / scant ½ cup whole buckwheat flour
60 g / ½ cup all-purpose flour*
1 Tbsp baking powder
½ tsp salt
1 tsp sugar
45 g / 3 Tbsp shortening, margarine, or butter
120 ml / ½ cup of milk (including milk substitutes such as nut or oat milks**)

* You can substitute the all-purpose flour here with all sorts of flours.

** If you have gluten-free flour, use it for a gluten-free dessert. Rye would be fun, as would Kamut or spelt. Non-dairy milks tend to be sweetened, so adjust accordingly.

Blueberry Grunt dumplings are steamed by the boiling berries below.

Seven Grain Sourdough Bread

Makes 1 large (9 × 4–inch loaf pan–sized) loaf

Equipment

9 × 4–inch bread pan
  OR Dutch oven
dough scraper

Ingredients

Sourdough Sponge

85 g / ½ cup and 3 Tbsp rye flour
85 ml / ⅓ cup and 1 Tbsp water
20 g (approx. 1 Tbsp) of starter

Final Dough

50 g / ⅓ cup buckwheat flour
50 g / ⅓ cup Kamut flour
50 g / ⅓ cup spelt flour
175 g / 1¼ cup whole wheat flour
175 ml / ¾ cup water
8 g salt

Seed Soaker

10 g / 1 Tbsp flax seeds
17 g / 2 Tbsp pumpkin seeds
17 g / 2 Tbsp sunflower seeds
75 g / ½ cup + 2 Tbsp oats
120 ml water

Exterior seed mix

1 tsp each of flax, pumpkin and
  sunflower seeds
3 Tbsp oats

Hydration

78%

've been making this bread almost every week since 2009. This recipe comes from the bakery I worked at in Germany, located on a beautiful farm named Dottenfelderhof. During my practicum, I worked alongside nine other dedicated bakers, often making over two thousand loaves of bread together in a night. I got such a rush and such joy from learning where to fit in with this highly competent crew of bakers, many of whom had practised the craft since they'd started apprenticeships at the of age sixteen.

This bread gives you flavour from all the whole-grain angles. With a good portion of wheat flour and the power of a rye sourdough, this dough will rise and give an open crumb. If you have different seeds than the ones indicated in the recipe, it's okay to swap or only use two of the three.

Consider this a "kitchen sink" recipe, where you keep the rye sourdough and ensure that a good portion of the final dough flour is wheat. This loaf makes excellent sandwich bread and really good toast, especially for a nut butter.

Ensure that your sourdough culture is lively. If necessary, refresh your sourdough culture at least the morning of, prior to mixing the overnight sponge (see page 33).

1. The day before you want to bake the bread, mix the 85 g of rye flour and water with your sourdough culture. Cover and let rest overnight on the counter.

2. In the morning, make your soaker by pouring 150 g water over the seeds and oats.

3. Mix the Sourdough Sponge and the Final Dough ingredients except the salt and the soaker in a bowl by hand or a mixer. It will feel rough, but keep mixing until it forms a fairly slack ball. Let rest for 30 minutes.

Add the salt and seed soaker and knead them in.

If using a mixer, mix these ingredients with the dough hook on a low speed for 6 minutes. You can skip the following resting and folding periods and move into the main bulk fermentation of the dough.

If working by hand, mix well, until the dough starts to become cohesive. Keep kneading the ingredients. It will be fairly sticky, so keep the dough in its bowl and knead it there, wetting your hands as needed to be able to engage with the dough more easily. Let the dough rest for 30 minutes.

continued...

4. Return to the dough and, using a dough scraper or your hand, turn it out onto a well-floured counter or tabletop. Flouring your own hands prior to handling the dough, flatten the ball into a disk by pressing down with your fingers. Then fold the outer 3 and 9 o'clock edges of the dough into the centre, pinching them in. Repeat this action, but bringing the 12 and 6 o'clock edges of the dough in this time. Repeat this folding method of kneading 6–10 times and return the dough to the bowl and cover. Use flour sparingly on the work surface and on your hands as needed to be able to handle the dough. Let rest for 30–45 minutes.

5. As you come back to the dough during the bulk fermentation, the dough should be starting to transform and becoming smoother. After 6–10 minutes of kneading, place the dough in a bowl or container.

Fold the dough like this one final time before leaving it for its final rest. Leave the dough to rest for 60 minutes in a warm place.

6. Mix the exterior seed mix (sunflower, pumpkin, and flax seeds, and oats) together in a bowl with a wide bottom or a plate with a lip.

7. For the final shaping, turn the dough out onto a floured work surface and follow the shaping for either a rectangular pan loaf or a round Dutch oven loaf.

If you want to make a rectangular loaf in a bread pan, take the kneaded dough ball and flatten it with your fingers. Fold the outside circle edges closest to your left and right hands into the middle, and then, from the top, tightly roll the rectangular dough disk into a log. Wet the dough either with your hands or by rolling on a pre-soaked, clean dishcloth. Roll the dough into the seed and oat mix. Place the loaf in a pan with the seam down, seeds up. Cover the pan to prevent your rising dough from drying out or regularly mist the top with a spray water bottle.

If you want to make a round loaf in a Dutch oven, find a soup bowl or smaller mixing bowl and line it with a flour-dusted cloth or tea towel. It will expand, so make sure the proofing vessel is large enough for that. Round the ball by hand, wet the top, and roll it around the seed mix. Then place the finished dough in a small, cloth-lined and floured bowl with the pinched dough pointed up, the smoothest side down.

8. Proof in a warm location for 40 minutes to 1 hour. Halfway through this final proof, turn the oven on to 205°C / 400°F and put the (empty) Dutch oven inside with the lid on if applicable.

9. After final proof, take your bread pan and score a few lines or a design with your sharpest knife. Cut no deeper than 1 cm. If you are baking the bread in a Dutch oven, remove the preheated baking dish from the oven with hand protection, remove the lid, and carefully invert the round proofed dough. Score the top and quickly put the lid on (with oven mitts) and return the Dutch oven to the oven. Leave the lid on for 15 minutes, then remove for the rest of the bake.

10. Bake the loaf pan for 45–50 minutes in the middle of the oven. If you have a thermometer, make sure the internal temperature has reached 93°C / 200°F.

11. Let cool for a few hours. If you must sample right out of the oven, tear it, don't try to cut it with a knife. Let it cure overnight at least, before sealing it in plastic to extend freshness.

Building the Oven

My time travelling across the United States—visiting my baking heroes and gaining a mentor or two—shaped my path for years to come. This is what a lot of bakers do: we share, we support, we make sure we can succeed. The baker's community has offered me courage to keep making space for Gold Island Bakery, to keep working towards a healthy, thriving bakery. Baking is a very demanding job that requires you to stay the course. I'm the student of many bakers from around the world. Many of my teachers are acknowledged in this book, as their lessons and recipes became part of mine. Tracing the recipes and techniques in this book will take you in many directions, to many locations, mapping the brilliance of bakers I've been fortunate to cross paths with.

But before I would know my strengths and how to use them, I had to learn the hard way.

My bakery resides in what I like to call my little sea can: a former shipping container retrofitted into a dream bread studio. The idea for a space like this came from a visit to iconic Vermont bakers and millwrights Blair Marvin and Andrew Heyn of Elmore Mountain Bread and New American Stone Mills. One summer while driving through New England, I stopped in and tented in the front yard of the bakery for the night. Tucked away in the hillside, sipping some craft beer after hours, we mused about the highs and lows of the baker's life. Blair mentioned how if she started over, she would think about building a shipping container bakery so that it could be moved to Santa Fe if they needed a big life change. My commitment to being in the Maritimes / Mi'kma'ki runs deep, so bakery portability wasn't a priority for me, but there were other good reasons to build a shipping container bakery. Basically, it meant building a ready-to-go, free-standing wood-fired asset for my future.

Building a bakery in a shipping container also seemed easier (and was cheaper) than creating a new building with a foundation. My research took me to a big lot in the local industrial park that specialized in selling new and used containers. Being on a budget (I was twenty-seven at the time and three years into running my little sourdough business), a manager of the container yard took me on a walk and we looked through a field of used containers. It was a simple choice that I based on the least amount of dents and a bit of intuition, and I picked out a cute, forest-green twenty-foot container. A few years prior I had started a co-op with some friends and together, we bought seventy-five acres of old farmland outside of Halifax/Kjipuktuk in a community called Scotch Village/Sipekne'katik. This was where my bakery would go.

On a trip to California, I sought out a woman named Lila Scott. Lila was the daughter of a well-known blacksmith and oven builder named Alan Scott, who had devoted much of his life to building community ovens and sharing as much knowledge as he could with fellow bakers. Even though he was gone, I was encountering his ovens and his name all over, even north of the border. Part of Allan's legacy, which his daughter Lila was carrying out, was keeping his oven designs available for purchase for people like me. There was a culture among rad bakers (read: engineer archetype) to build your own oven. Maybe I could too. It wasn't long after getting home from my roadtrip to California that I started to plan out what kind of bakery I would eventually have, and ordered Alan Scott oven plans.

I knew the smallest commercial Alan Scott oven would be right for me after my friend and baking mentor Doug Brown offered to let me bake in his. He had actually ordered Allan Scott plans himself years prior, and hired a mason to build the very oven I was considering. Alas, the local mason didn't have the skill to build arches, so Doug completed the oven on his own. If Doug could, maybe I could too?

Doug had invited me to come by on a Friday after he had finished his own market bake, so that I could bake for my own Saturday market. This seemed like an incredible opportunity to help inform my decision. Despite recognizing some peak Chaos Ross decision-making rising in me, I woke up unusually early one morning to mix my sourdough buckets so they would be ripe by late afternoon and primed for baking at the appointed time. Midday I packed up the car and drove the two hours down the valley to Doug's dreamy wood-fired-oven bakery.

Called Oak Haven, Doug's bakery is attached to his house, just outside of a small town called Bridgetown. Not only did I have my sourdough buckets in tow that day, but I had bags of flour, special ingredients, and the bread pans needed to make my normal goods. My operation had gone mobile, all packed into a Honda Civic. It was a laborious yet fruitful experiment. The small Alan Scott commercial design was a great fit for the scale of production I had grown into over the years. I was never more easily able to imagine my life as a wood-fired baker as I was that evening, making the tired trip back to Halifax/Kjipuktuk ahead of the early-morning Saturday market.

Enthused and ambitious, I slowly sourced all the materials for the oven on the piece of land that I co-owned with friends. Despite all the anxiety one would have when starting a project like this, I got as far as pouring a concrete pad for the eventual oven. The next step was starting to build the cinder block foundation. Surrounded by two friends, I attempted to mix the first of many unique mortars needed to build a wood-fired oven. A hard realization came over my ambitious spirit: I may have purchased the materials, but I was struggling through the

Younger Jess still getting familiar with her new oven and space.

But I didn't know how to make this goal a reality. I was devastated. Mid-cinder foundation, I quit. This part of my baker's life was pivotal, a moment of failure.

I don't let go of things easily, even when they don't serve me. Thankfully, I knew of a German mason in the province named Volker Klum. My failure pivoted towards a reward: I could still have my skillfully made wood-fired oven. Foregoing my own ambitions to follow in the footsteps of other bakers who build their own ovens—a fairly common practice—I brought on a professional in the form of Volker. The oven he would craft for me is still as strong and functional as that first day I lit a fire in it ten years ago.

The first time I fired my oven to bake, my shipping container bakery was an empty space with some shelving and a folding table. I didn't yet have a mixer or even a door. It would take years to legitimize my baking studio into a commercial kitchen. It was a fairly solitary journey with a lot of help from my friends. One benefit that came from the snails-pace cultivation of my little dream bakery was getting to work in an unmoulded space, to figure out just the right tools and infrastructures that a very small workspace needed. The process of building my own bakery in a little shipping container bakery to its eventual commercial certification was long, with many hurdles. Logistical fails, administrative blocks, the crossing of all the proverbial Ts of the provincial food safety bureaucracy, and the weight of many a bag of poorly poured concrete almost broke me. But then, there was glory and joy in finally being able to bake my very own sourdough recipes in my very own wood-fired oven.

earliest stages of my emerging scrappy masonry career. Building a brick oven involves strategic combinations of powder, aggregate, and water. Ironically, the skill of a mortar-mixing mason is not unlike the skill of a dough-mixing baker. Just very different kinds of ingredients. But my baking skills were apparently not comparable or translatable to masonry skills. I had to accept feelings of deficiency, even as I embraced that I actually wanted these thousands of dollars of materials to become an oven that would last.

Top: Jess's wood-fired oven.

Bottom: Jess's "little sea can" shipping-container bakery.

WHEAT
(Triticum aestivum)

Wheat is such a crucial grain to so many humans. Its origins are considered instrumental to the birth of agriculture. Wheat flour is one of the most common ingredients found in the kitchens of the world, if not the most common. Wheat in itself is a whole realm of grain diversity. It also has an incredibly rich history as a food and plant that has roamed the planet, joining the unnecessary division of the western and eastern world.

GEOGRAPHICAL ORIGIN & ERA OF EMERGENCE: Wheat was first farmed around 10,000 years ago in parts of the Levantine Valle, in what is now Jordan, Syria, and West Bank–Palestine.

HISTORICAL IMPORTANCE: Wheat moved north and west from the Levant, growing commonly in Northern Africa by 6,000 BC, where the first oven and bread cultures emerged in Egypt. Wheat continued its journey, moving with humans to other parts of Asia, Spain, Germany, and then the British isles. It wasn't until European colonialism that wheat crossed the Atlantic. Canada's wheat industry is a lasting consequence of the British Empire's focus on wheat within its agricultural colonialism. As Britain forced its frontier west across this land, into the prairies, farms to grow and railways to move wheat took over. Perennial grasslands managed since time immemorial by Indigenous Plains Peoples (like the Niitsitapi, or Blackfoot, and Nêhiyawak, or Cree) were converted into massive tracts of slowly depleting farmland. Canada's wheat production would even impact the UK in that Canadian wheat was often cheaper and higher in protein than wheat grown on British soil, leading to the decline of centuries of landrace varieties of wheat.

FLAVOUR: nutty, grassy/hay, mellow bitterness.

SPECIAL FEATURES: Wheat feeds billions of people every day in all kinds of ways! It is also incredibly adaptive, with all kinds of regionally specific varieties that are suited to their local microclimates and culinary customs. *Triticum aestivum* (bread wheats and spelt) and *Triticum durum* (semolina wheats for pasta and bulgur) are the most common wheats grown and consumed today. Other ancient varieties of wheat you may know of are emmer, einkorn, and Khorasan or Kamut. When milled whole, it is very nutritious, yielding vitamins, minerals, dietary fibre, and various amino acids. When fermented through the cultivation of bacteria and wild yeasts (sourdough), it yields a more easily digested food that is also delicious.

CHALLENGES: The story of wheat today is no longer a story of breaking bread or our agrarian roots, but has become a symbol of monoculture in the fields—and one of the most chemically sprayed foods we consume. It's common practice in conventional agriculture to spray wheat fields with the herbicide glyphosate (also known as Roundup) so that all the plants start drying simultaneously once the spray hits the grasses. The appetite for wheat in North America has led to various agricultural practices that are both ecologically and economically fraught. The vast majority of that wheat is grown for the production of all-purpose/white flour, which is stripped of the vast majority of its nutritional value as a food, found in the bran and the germ, leaving only the endosperm. This makes white or all-purpose flour the standard and most accessible form of flour and wheat for much of the western world.

In terms of baking, I appreciate white flour being so standardized that our baking results are so similar. But white flour being the standard also means that fewer bakers have the know-how necessary to bake with whole-grain wheat flours. This is because the bran and germ can prevent gluten bonds in the dough from forming. However, by adding water amounts that soften the grain just right (more than you would for white flour) you can maximize whole wheat flour's gluten potential.

Clockwise: soft wheat bran, whole farro kernels, conventional whole wheat flour, hard wheat bran, medium bulgur, artisanal steel-ground whole wheat flour, and hard wheat kernels (centre).

BEST USES: So many of the baked goods we know and love worldwide are founded on the performance of wheat gluten. If you are looking to convert a favourite white flour recipe that involves significant rising or aeration to a whole-grain recipe, experimenting with whole wheat flours is easier than you think. Using a fine sieve can allow you to sift off the largest pieces of bran that may interfere with your desire for a lofty finished baked good. But don't throw them away—keep excess bran in the fridge or freezer for bread or muffins, where the oils that give the grain flavour can stay fresh and flavourful.

TRIVIA: Grain breeding is responsible for many of wheat's advantageous characteristics, like having no hull. Over millennia, cultivated wheats became domesticated because they lost their ability to self-seed in the wild. Humans would have gathered wheat by hand; the stalks (also called *rachis*) with loose kernels would have dropped easier, and those that held on would have stayed with the harvester and been more likely to be planted out the following year, propagating that particular trait.

The Wild Side

t all starts with a spark. The paper catches first. A blow of air on crumpled, used buttery parchment is all it takes to set it off what builds and then dwindles. The chain reaction starts, paper to boxboard to bark bits and then to oven-dried slab wood, to catch and burn hardwood logs, the ones who carry most of the energy to bake inside of them. Over the cycle of a firing, the wood-fired oven crackles with a range of snaps, bursts, and spits. For me, tending fire to make bread is a nurturing practice, a ritual to remind me of the basics: light, heat, transformation, circulation, store, and release.

I was jumping into the deep end with the bare minimum amount of experience in dealing with a wood-fired oven on my own. No teachers or mentors on-site, the final responsibility my own. Navigating this learning curve involved a lot of lost sleep, chaotic and lonely baking sessions full of big feels and often big disappointments.

However, with each bake I moved closer to balancing the burning of wood with the timing of making, shaping, and ultimately baking bread dough. Making eight different kinds of bread within each bake, some loaves would be spot on and others would be off. It required a daily calibration of my time, my fire, my sourdough starters, and myself. It is still a reality for me, and regular missteps happen alongside regular victories, yet they always yield some damn delicious wood-fired baked bread. But before there were impeccable loaves coming out of my wood-fired oven, there were many burnt loaves.

Leading up to actually having my own wood-fired oven, I had the opportunity to experiment and work with a few. In Germany I was lucky to work at the Dottenfelderhof bakery, which had three wood-fired ovens. The bakery started off small, decades ago, with just one oven. As the farm and bakery grew, new wood-fired ovens were added while the old ones were maintained. There were two small commercial direct-fire ovens right on the oven floor, where the loaves baked later in the shift. The final and newest oven was a relatively sophisticated blend of new and old technology. It was a triple-deck, steam injector–equipped, indirect-fire oven. It had a separate firebox below the decks so the baker could load wood as needed throughout the bake to boost or maintain desired heat. Together, these ovens represented the changing eras of this beautiful workspace, and helped us make over a thousand loaves each bake.

By the end of my practicum on Dottenfelderhof, I had been given the responsibility of tending to the fire, cleaning out the ash, and loading the middle oven, which was a small, direct-fire oven, similar in size to the one I would eventually have. It was the oven whose only job during the shift was to bake one or two big batches of one of my favourite breads, siebenkornbrot (seven grain bread). Siebenkornbrot is a nutty, grainy, free-form, round, whole-grain sourdough loaf made up of all the grains found within the bakery. It's a loaf I would later make in my own wood-fired oven, one that is still being made by Gold Island bakers.

Unlike modern gas or electric ovens, wood-fired ovens heat up very slowly over many hours. The fire infuses the oven with a sustained blast of radiant heat over a 4-hour burn cycle, storing enough energy for 6 hours of continuous baking. Becoming a wood-fired-oven baker means learning some fundamentals about the nature of energy transformation. Being a sourdough baker also asks this of us. The scientist part of me thrived in slowly figuring out the nuances of the burn from each different type of wood, learning to calibrate the amount of wood to the size of the bake.

The free-form wheat doughs are the very first to go in the oven. These loaves are full of springing potential, and the brutish early heat of the oven is essential in helping the loaves rise properly. It also has the potential to make the most of these loaves or ruin them. The way these wheat hearth loaves react and shade with colour as they bake towards completion says a lot about how the rest of the session is going to go. It's a quick study as they undergo the fastest transition from dough to loaf, baking in under 20 minutes, sometimes as fast as twelve. How quickly the wheat crusts brown after 10 minutes tells me how long it's going to take the scones to finish, even though they won't go in the oven for another 3 hours.

But beyond the visual cues, there are deeply olfactory ones as well. This is where the sesame wheat loaves come in. They are the canaries of the bake; they tell the truth of the fire, no secrets or coverups. The aromas that come from a perfectly roasted sesame whole wheat hearth loaf are expansive, and the intensity of their aroma, as well as their development, can tell you so much. The near burnt crust pushes the flavour realm towards bitterness, the sweetness of the sesame holding it back. From top to bottom and end to end of that loaf, there is a visual and flavour range available to you, signalled by its colours, from just-baked golden to almost-burnt garnet. There's an instability inherent in baking these delicately dotted loaves with a wood-fired oven, and occasionally my approach brings me to question the place of these loaves in a commercial bake. Always baking on my own, I've gone somewhat unchecked. On burnt-bottomed or side-cracked days, I sometimes consider cutting them from our roster, but the

taste is just so good and they always sell out. I love that the hearth loaves carry more of the flavour of the smoky stone, the oven itself, their crusts spending the most time directly against the stone. Something extra, something of me, my practice, my journey here.

The variability and free nature of working with whole grains and fire requires constant learning for us bakers. Learning the magic of whole-grain baking shows us how to love all the parts: bran, germ, and endosperm. I'm deeply devoted to whole grains. Whole-grain baking articulates my embrace of non-normativity, my queerness, and radical lessons divergent from the status quo. I work to honour the methods of my teachers and embrace my wild side and the wild nature of existence, as I also work to honour the true spontaneity and non-conformity of nature.

Baking with whole grains reminds us to tune in, to feel, to look, and to taste everything, even raw dough. Alongside all the instability, diligent repetition through bread baking cultivates responsiveness, making for oven magic. Each bake is like a long dance, a sequence of moves and mixes on repeat alongside the variables of life. As I bake for a community, they experience the range of my recipes. They hear from the chatty baker at the market preaching about how the results of a bake are determined by factors like the conditions in the field. They learn how grain is stored once harvested, about the milling of the flour, the capacities of the baker, the fundamental spontaneity of a living grain and culture paired with someone carrying the nickname Chaos Ross.

Whole Wheat Brown Bread

Makes 1 large loaf

As mentioned in the recipe for Anadama Sourdough Bread (page 70), older brown bread recipes were made with whole grains, their flours coarser and stone-ground, the colour and caramel sweetness of the breads coming from thick molasses. Brown breads would have been steamed in pots or tins rather than baked in home ovens. Today, most brown breads are a shadow of their former selves. And that's unfortunate because brown breads are workhorses and beauties all at once.

To be fair, I find commercially-available brown bread has such a comforting taste—and I know many others feel this way too—but that doesn't mean there can't be a middle ground. This loaf is a kid-friendly and yeasted whole wheat bread that is texturally similar to our more modern interpretation of brown bread, but with a touch more flavour. It's modified from a recipe that was published by Crosby's Molasses, a 150-year-old sugar-processing company which is now based in one of my hometowns, Saint John, New Brunswick. That very brand of molasses was a staple condiment on our kitchen table, in my grandmother's baking pantry, and remains one for many a Maritimer to this day.

Oats, whole wheat, molasses, yeast, and salt make this delicious and easy recipe, tailor-made for poached eggs and baked beans or just served with a good spread of salted butter or margarine.

Equipment
large loaf pan
    (approx. 9 × 4 inches)
        OR Dutch oven
flexible dough scraper

Ingredients
120 ml / ½ cup warm water
1½ tsp dry active yeast

90g / ⅓ cup molasses
50g / ½ cup oats (old-fashioned,
    preferably not instant)
15g / 1 Tbsp butter
7g / 1 tsp salt
120 ml / ½ cup boiling water
60 ml / ¼ cup cold water
360 g / 3 cups whole wheat flour

1. Start by mixing ½ cup warm water with the yeast. Set aside in a small bowl for 5–10 minutes.

2. Meanwhile, in a large bowl, add molasses, oats, butter, salt, and pour boiling water over these ingredients. Stir until the butter is dissolved and the ingredients are mixed. Let sit for a few minutes.

3. Add the cold water to the molasses mix and stir in. Next, add in the yeast mix and the pre-measured flour into the bowl.

4. Mix everything together by hand and knead in the bowl (with wet hands if necessary) until the dough becomes less shaggy and becomes more uniform. Once the dough is in a nice ball shape, let it rest for 15–20 minutes.

5. When you return to the dough after this first rest, knead it by hand and/or with a flexible dough scraper in the bowl. Keeping a bowl of water around to dip your hand in occasionally is really helpful here. Just be careful not to mix too much water in. The dough texture should get noticeably wetter. Knead the dough for at least 5 minutes by hand. (Take breaks as needed.)

6. Place rounded dough back in a large bowl. Take a small amount of butter, margarine, or oil onto your hands. Melt between your hands and massage over top of the dough ball. Cover the bowl with a damp cloth or a lid to proof in a warm spot for 1 hour. It should have almost doubled in size or at least be significantly risen.

   (If you're looking for a possible proofing chamber to help your loaf, turn your oven onto its lowest heat setting before starting to knead. Once preheated, turn off.

7. Turn the dough onto a floured counter or table. Fold or knead the dough to degas.

8. Leave in a covered bowl for 20 minutes. Place the dough ball on a flour-dusted surface and flatten the circle of dough by spreading out your fingers and pressing the dough down, turning it into a wide disk less than 1 inch tall.

Proofed dough ready to be shaped.

Folding the edges in to make a triangle.

Pinning the point of the triangle down.

Tucking and rolling the dough tightly for final log shape.

9. Fold in the sides of the disk toward the middle, making it narrower at the top and wider at the bottom, like a wedge or pizza slice. Tuck the top narrow part in, and start rolling the dough towards yourself while tucking it tightly in until you have a dough log. With the seam facing down, place it in an oiled bread pan.

10. Let it rise for 30 minutes, then turn on the oven to 160°C / 325°F. Rub the top of the loaf in 1 tsp of butter or shortening. Next sprinkle with lots of oats and gently press them in. When the oven is preheated, score your loaf by cutting a pattern no deeper than 1 cm.

11. Bake at 160°C / 325°F for 1 hour. Remove from the pan and let cool for a few hours before slicing.

Whole Wheat Oatmeal Raisin Cookies

Makes 36 cookies

Equipment
whisk

Ingredients

Dry
330 g / 3 cups oats

175g / 1 cup brown sugar (or white sugar plus 1 tsp of molasses)

225g / 1 cup soft butter (or shortening, margarine or a blend)

130 g / 1 cup whole wheat flour

1 tsp baking soda

225g / 1½ cups raisins (or chocolate chips, toasted pumpkin seeds, nut chunks, or a combination thereof)

Wet
2 eggs

30 ml / 2 Tbsp hot water

NOTE: If you are making these cookies by hand, ensure the butter is soft and the eggs are at room temperature before starting.

Both wheat and oats are naturally sweet, and when combined they create a flavoursome cookie that will change the way you view whole grains. In this Whole Wheat Oatmeal Raisin Cookie recipe, sweet bursts of raisins balance the grain-forward nuttiness, but if you're feeling the need for chocolate, the same amount of chocolate chips will do the trick.

This recipe is an adaptation of a prize-winning oatmeal raisin cookie featured in the *Saint Croix Courier,* a newspaper in Charlotte County, New Brunswick. It uses baking soda dissolved in hot water as a leavener, a technique that also appears in the Maritime Oatcakes recipe (see page 58). A nice choice for the cookie jar, these cookies keep well for up to 2 weeks. Alternatively, they can be frozen very fresh for a future cool cookie treat.

1. Mix butter, eggs, sugar, and water in a bowl together with a whisk or electric beaters. Cream these ingredients together by vigorously mixing the bowl contents until they are homogeneous and airy.

2. In a medium bowl, mix all the dry ingredients *except* the raisins. Sift or whisk these ingredients.

3. With a rubber spatula, add the creamed mix to the dry, folding it all together. Once blended, add in the raisins.

4. Preheat oven to 190°C / 375°F.

5. Line a cookie sheet with parchment paper or use a non-stick tray. Make 12 cookies per sheet and drop spoonfuls of dough onto the tray. Once the oven is preheated, bake cookies for approximately 12 minutes or until golden.

6. Transfer to a cooling rack or other surface to cool before storing in an airtight container.

Rustic Pancakes

Makes about 8 pancakes

Pancakes are a nice way to change a morning routine into something special, and whole-grain pancakes are probably the easiest way to introduce the flavours of whole grains to your friends and family. This recipe uses baking soda and the lactic acid found in yogurt reaction to give an extra rise and a nice tang.

These pancakes are also a great teacher, in that you can really begin to see how each grain (and its respective flour) absorbs liquid, as well as how much. All you need to remember is that you want a dough that is wet enough so it spreads out for a few seconds when the batter hits the hot pan. The amount of milk listed in this recipe should get you close to that, but depending on the flour, you may need more.

I love to prepare a fruit side to go along with pancakes. Maybe you have some berries you could quickly cook with a sweetener and a leaf of basil? Or you can serve these with yogurt, apple sauce, and maple syrup alongside some maple and bacon.

1. Combine all the dry ingredients and whisk well together in a medium-large bowl.

2. Whisk the egg, milk, and yogurt together. Next, whisk in the melted butter.

3. Add the wet mix into the dry and stir until just well combined using a rubber spatula or big wooden spoon.

4. Turn a frying pan or cast iron onto medium heat. When you think the pan is ready, drop a small pat of butter into the pan. When the butter sizzles quickly, you can start frying the pancakes. Add butter between every or every other round of pancakes.

5. Pour ¼ cup of batter at a time into your pan. Once the cakes have fully risen and the underside is golden, flip the pancakes. The second side doesn't take as long as the first.

6. Serve with fruit, butter or margarine, and maple syrup.

Equipment
frying pan

Ingredients
Dry

195 g / 1½ cups whole wheat flour (this recipe should work with most whole-grain flours)

1 Tbsp baking powder

½ tsp baking soda

1 Tbsp sugar

½ tsp salt

Wet

1 large egg

180 to 240 ml / ¾–1 cup milk, or non-dairy milk 125g / ½ cup yogurt (or DIY buttermilk, page 48)

30 ml / 2 tablespoons butter, melted

NOTE: This batter can be made ahead of time and refrigerated for up to 12 hours, but should be made a little bit extra wet, as a lot of the liquid will be absorbed into the batter over time and it will stiffen. Bring back to room temperature before using.

Sprouted Grain Mincemeat

Makes around 1 L

ooking back through my Nan's recipes, it's clear to see how mincemeat has adapted from a spiced, chunky, meat-centric pie filling to a spiced, dried fruit, booze, and citrus concoction. Mincemeat may have changed, but it still references the flavour and textures of older versions (often made with animal products), while being vegetarian.

Newer iterations involve less labour, less cooking time, and avoid now hard-to-find ingredients like suet. In this Sprouted Grain Mincemeat adaptation, I maintain the primary traditional elements of aromatic alcohols, preserved orange and lemon, apple, dried fruits for a meaty mouthfeel, as well as seasonings and sweeteners such as molasses, cinnamon, cloves, nutmeg, and pepper. In a note from Nan's mincemeat-from-scratch recipe, she mentions using ground beef. This pebbly texture, I realized after some contemplation, could be mimicked with the chewy bite of sprouted whole kernels of different grains like rye, wheat, or spelt. Here, I offer you my spiced and sprouted grain morsel mincemeat.

DAYS 1–3

1. Soak the dried grain kernels with cold water in a 1 L mason jar for 1 hour. You want just enough water to completely cover them. Turn this vessel into your sprouting jar by placing cheesecloth on the top of the jar and fixing with a mason-jar ring. Drain the water from the jar in the sink by inverting and holding for 1 minute. Next, leave the jar tilted in a bowl upside down so excess water can drain. That night, rinse and drain again, leaving it tilted overnight. Repeat this in the morning and evening, always using cool water. Do this for a third and final day. By soaking and draining the kernels repeatedly, we are activating the seed and causing it to germinate.

DAY 4

2. On the 4th day, transfer the sprouting grain into a strainer, rinse well, and let drain thoroughly.

3. Chop the apricots and dates finely. Clean and zest the citrus. Assemble your ground spice mix in a medium mixing bowl. Add the zest and rum. Mix in the grain and dried fruit. Stir this well and pack in an airtight container, and store in a cool place. Shake or stir every few days and leave for 1–2 weeks.

AFTER 1–2 WEEKS

4. When you are ready to finish, bring the applesauce, sugar, and molasses to a boil and cook on low for 5 minutes. Turn off and stir in the brandy.

5. Pour this mix into a bowl and add the rum-soaked grain and fruit. Mash it up a bit. Pack this mix in containers and freeze it for later use, or store it in jars in the fridge for up to 1 month. This mincemeat makes a perfect tart filling for Whole Grain Pie Pastry (see page 88) or can be used in any other mincemeat recipes.

Ingredients
90 g / ½ cup wheat berries
80 g / ½ cup oat groats
90 g / ½ cup rye kernels
90 g / ½ cup chopped dates
85 g / ½ cup chopped apricots
75 g / ½ cup raisins
zest of 1 lemon
zest of 1 orange
150 ml spiced rum

Ground Spices
1 tsp nutmeg
1 tsp cloves
1 tsp cinnamon
1 tsp black pepper
60 g / ¼ cup brown or cane sugar
60 ml / ¼ cup molasses
380g / 1½ cups applesauce
2 shots brandy or other aromatic
    booze on hand

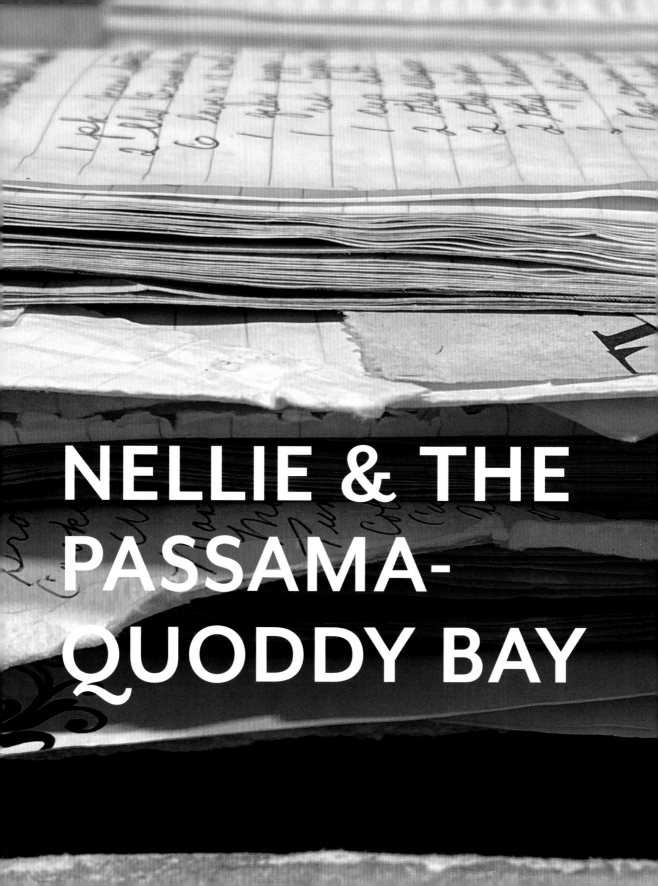

NELLIE & THE PASSAMA-QUODDY BAY

've spent much of my life living on Mi'kmaq territory, a name I learned only as I entered adulthood. Over the years, I've changed the way I name home. For me this is about honouring the land I consider home, drawing buried histories into the present, and acknowledging the people, the plants, and the places that have stewarded this land: land that grows grain, holds water to drink, and sustains so much life.

For me, alternative grain growing is a way to help free the land of capitalist toxicity. So is acknowledging the long Indigenous ancestry of the land that grows the grain. Unceded Mi'kma'ki territory includes both of my homelands, New Brunswick and Nova Scotia, the former my birthplace and the latter my current home. Next to Mi'kma'ki is Peskotomuhkati territory (English name: Passamaquoddy). I grew up knowing it as Charlotte County, New Brunswick, the very southeast corner of Canada. I haven't lived there since I was four when my mom, Jennifer, moved us closer to a city, but I don't ache for any place the way I ache for Charlotte County.

My ancestors have lived there, in the Northeast Atlantic, as settlers for over five generations. My great-grandparents worked seasonally in Boston, like many a Maritimer at the time, but settled just on the other side of the US border in New Brunswick. The European origins of my family lineages are numerous, reaching back to places across the Atlantic I can't name. Charlotte County is the only place I can visit knowing that my ancestors lived and died there. Our most important family recipes lead back there. It's where I started my life, where my grandparents lie. I am rooted to this place, especially the water that encompasses much of Charlotte County, the Passamaquoddy Bay. Many of my favourite memories involve scavenging for smooth, bright beach glass, or mermaid's tears as we called them. We combed for these, alongside searching for crabs in the ankle-deep tide pools, revealed by the outgoing and long tidespan of the Bay of Fundy.

No matter how long I've been gone, Charlotte County feels like home. When I arrived in May of 2022 for a research trip devoted to this project, my body was still tense with the energy of having driven nearly six hours after a flight from Toronto/Tkaronto. I had been driving non-stop so I could make a late-afternoon Zoom meeting, arriving in St. Andrews/ Qonasqamkuk with about forty minutes to spare after unloading the car. It was just enough time to make bodily contact with the shore, and the waters of Passamaquoddy Bay.

Touching the bay is one of my main landing rituals when I arrive here. It starts with taking my socks off, dried crunchy seaweed immediately underfoot. My feet, fresh out of shoes, chill quickly from the brisk May temperature. It is the first time I've hit the beach this season, getting sanded as I head to the shoreline. Next up, feet in the water, pant legs hiked as high as they can. A seasoned polar swimmer, the rush of a spring bayside body immersion is like a drug for me. It is an instant grounding, a body awareness spurred on by shocking my system as I submerge my nerves into the frigid, enclosing sharpness of the cold. It is the kind of presence perfect for baking, actually.

I have come to this place to write, and in order to write, I must take walks. The movement, fresh air, and birdsong grounds me. They help me sort ideas and think of words to describe the connections I feel between baking, caretaking, work ethics, and a livable future full of whole grains. I've been thinking a lot about this lately, not just because of this book, my career, but more so this place. During one late-morning work break, a walk took me along a newer pathway in St. Andrews. The path wrapped around the shore of the Passamaquoddy Bay, commonly referred to as The Point and known by the Indigenous peoples here as Qonasqamkuk (translates to "at the sandy point"). Taking the path, across the water I saw different landmarks of Chamcook, Deer Island, and L'Etete, places that held my family and carry our history. This trip was a reconciliation of the past with my

present, as is this book. Over the years much of my family has scattered or passed on. To keep Charlotte County and the Bay close in my heart, I hold a tradition of returning at least once a year.

This visit, I'm focused on family recipes— revisiting my relatives and the foods they made and shared together, memorialized in my late grandmother's recipe notebook. My Nan, Jean Anne Stevens, nee MacGillvray, left her cookbooks to me upon her passing in 2019. When she died, this cookbook was already in motion and her recipes, alongside others, were always meant to be a part of it. But since she died, the inclusion of Jean's recipes have taken on new meaning, as have reading through and baking many of the recipes she collected over the years and then left to me.

Jean cited her recipes diligently. Almost every one of the four hundred or so recipes that she had pasted or written out into a coil notebook had an author listed. Only one recipe, War Cake (a cake made with little to no butter or refined sugar, made for war rationing), came from Nellie, my great-grandmother who I never met, but who's memory lived near the surface of our family psyche. Nellie Mabel MacGillivray was born in Green Point, New Brunswick, in 1895, and passed away close by in St. Andrews in 1980, five years before I was born. She was my mother's mother's mother. I decided to start with her.

It's hard to say what my grandmother's relationship to her own mother was, though by piecing together family history and reading between the lines, I know it wasn't easy. Nellie's daughter Jean's recipe collection didn't offer me much insight into their dynamic or Nellie's own culinary traditions. It was only when I helped clean out my grandmother's apartment after her passing that I could put a little bit more together. I found and kept a scrapbook of Nellie's, filled with cards, news clippings, and material memories, giving me glimpses into her world before my time.

On this May visit to Charlotte County, Nellie was more present for me than usual. Returning to her home brought me closer to the lived paths of my matriarchs, showing me the roads, shores, and vistas that would have been a part of their lives in Chamcook. I learned that Nellie and her sister, Eva Cleopatra, were orphaned young, to be raised by family legend Sea Captain Hines and his family. I learned that the Hines family, including Nellie and Eva, were the lighthouse keepers at Green Point, just across the bay from where I would walk during my writing days. Nellie would have spent a lot of her time on these shores then.

Nellie was widowed suddenly with eight children when she was thirty-seven. At the time my Nan, Jean Anne, was five years old. Nellie's War Cake recipe signals a time of particular austerity, including when it came to baking ingredients. Some of our family recipes are, at first glance, symbols of hardship, yet they give me access to family joy. Keeping these family recipes alive, or even just documented, was a way for Jean to connect to home through her years as a grandmother, and also for me as an adult living far from this place. The recipes in this next section are whole-grain adaptations of recipes I grew up with, as well as others I found in my grandmother's collection after her passing. They all tell a small piece of the story of home, a story of Charlotte County, of settler histories, of family foods.

On this visit home, my mom and I were able to track down the piece of land where the house Jean was born in stood. We did this with Google Maps, the help of some old photographs, and a live phone consultation with my grandmother's last living sibling in Ontario, my great-uncle

Everett MacGillvray. At the time, I was already deep into baking my grandmother's recipes, making adaptations of them. With my baking research practice, I wanted to both visit the recipes as they were and also to bring the recipes forward into my time and baking style. Before this trip I had been boldly experimenting with the War Cake recipe concept. I brought some of Nellie's War Cake with me from Ontario, both her version and mine, wrapped and packed in my suitcase. On this day, while sleuthing and searching, I had those War Cakes with me. When we found the location of Nellie's old house, I took that cake, crushed it by hand, and sprinkled its crumbs atop the scrubby land. This place was no longer a house or even a foundation, but I felt connected.

War Cake (War is Over)

Makes 1 large 2-tiered cake

This is a wild adaptation of the only recipe authored by my great grandmother Nellie in all six hundred of her recipes. The original recipe harkens to a time of austerity during the world wars, when raisins were a more available cake sweetener than sugar.

This War Cake recipe (created by a libra) interprets war less literally, instead thinking about the balance of death and growth, of earth and flowers, and how they relate to each other. A surprising base of nettle cake supports a spongy rose and raspberry top half, all enrobed in buttercream and decorated with textures, colours, and flavours to confuse and engage the senses. Nettles, a spring plant, both hurt and heal. The same can be said for summer roses and raspberries, thorny and sweet. Of course, you can also make this recipe if you aren't interested in casting a spell, but want to make a showstopper dessert that tells a visual and flavourful story of roses and thorns.

Make this recipe to cast a spell for intergenerational healing.

Equipment
icing gear (piping bag, floral tip)
electric mixer for buttercream
fine mesh sieve/sifter
food processor (for nettle)

Ingredients for all components combined
250 ml raspberry jam
food colouring (green [or blue or yellow], red or pink)
fondant (at least 1 cup)
680 g / 3 cups butter plus a few Tbsp
800 g / 4 cups sugar
½ cup raisins
5 cups whole spelt flour
11 eggs
15 ml / 3 tsp vanilla
45 ml / 3 Tbsp lemon juice
rind from ½ a lemon
4½ tsp baking powder
2 cups fresh or dried nettles
10 ml / 2 tsp rosewater
optional: rose petals

NOTE: This steps of this recipe are separated into days for purely functional purposes. If you can organize yourself to make it all in one day, bless you. But I find this way to be the easiest way to manage my time, and my expectations.

DAY 1

1. Prepare your spelt flour, passing it through a fine mesh sieve, removing the largest bran flakes. You should be taking away only a couple of tablespoons of bran. (You can save this for a muffin or bread recipe.) You will need just under 5 cups total flour for the 2 cakes.

2. Make the Buttercream.

A. Put a medium saucepan with a few inches of water on to boil.

B. In a separate bowl, whisk the sugar and egg whites together. Place the bowl over the simmering pot of water and continue to whisk, creating a double boiler. Whisk until you can no longer feel any granules of sugar.

C. Once the sugar is dissolved, remove the pot from heat. Wipe away any moisture from the exterior of the bowl to ensure none gets in your buttercream. Using a stand or hand mixer, whip the whites and sugar until the mix is foaming and shiny. Continue to whip until it roughly doubles in size.

D. Once the whip is doubled and looks like a shiny meringue, start adding small pieces of butter, one at a time. Keep mixing, and add butter only as the previous addition becomes homogenous with the meringue and is fully integrated.

E. Keep mixing like this until the butter is mixed and the buttercream starts to smooth out. This may take longer than you think, so don't worry if it looks curdled at first. Have patience and keep mixing. It will smoothen out. Once you've finished adding butter and the buttercream looks voluminous and smooth, it's done.

F. Split the buttercream in half. Mix one half with green food colouring and the other with pink, between 4 to 8 drops in each. In the pink one, add 1 tsp / 5 ml of rosewater. Set aside or refrigerate until you are close to assembly time.

3. Make the Raisin Caramel Crunch.

A. Melt the butter in a medium saucepan.

B. Add the sugar and cook on medium for 4 minutes, stirring occasionally.

Buttercream ingredients
200 g / 1 cup sugar
4 egg whites, room temperature
368 g / 1⅔ cup unsalted butter, room temperature.
5 ml / 1 tsp vanilla

Raisin Caramel Crunch Ingredients
115 g / ½ cup butter
100 g / ½ cup sugar
75 g / ½ cup raisins

C. Add the raisins and continue to cook, turning the heat down to medium-low and stirring regularly, for another 5 minutes. It should darken slightly, a nice soft blond.

D. Pour onto a cookie sheet, lined with parchment or wax paper. Refrigerate and allow to cool completely.

E. Once hardened, transfer onto a cutting board and chop into small slivers.

Lemon Nettle Cake
Ingredients
2 packed cups of fresh nettles (If unable to find fresh, 3 cups of dried nettles will do)

125 ml / ½ cup boiling water (if using dried)

45 ml / 3 Tbsp lemon juice

15 / 1 Tbsp lemon zest

325g / 2⅔ cup sifted spelt flour

2½ tsp baking powder

227 g / 1 cup butter, room temperature

200 g / 1 cup sugar

4 eggs, room temperature

5 ml / 1 tsp vanilla

DAY 2

1. Make the Lemon Nettle Cake.

1A. Prepare the nettles. Using gloves to protect your hands from the stinging nettles, blanch them in boiling water for 20 seconds or so. *If using dried nettles,* pour a ½ cup of boiling water over the dried nettles and allow to sit for a few minutes. Strain the nettles, pressing gently to squeeze out any excess liquid. Purée in a food processor or mince finely with a knife. Set aside.

1B. Combine the lemon zest and lemon juice in a small bowl and set aside.

1C. Preheat the oven to 175°C / 350°F. Grease and then line a 10-inch springform pan with parchment.

1D. Sift the baking powder and flour together. Set aside.

1E. Cream the butter and sugar together by using a mixer or whisking by hand for 3–5 minutes. You want the creamed butter and sugar to be pale and fluffy.

1F. Add the eggs one at a time, mixing each one in as you go. Scrape down the sides of the bowl after each egg. When all the eggs are added, continue mixing for another minute.

1G. Add the vanilla and mix well, followed by the lemon juice and zest.

1H. Finally mix in the nettle (either the fresh purée or the moistened dried nettle).

1I. Add the flour to your cake batter, mix just until fully combined. Transfer batter into the springform pan and place in preheated oven.

1J. Bake for 25–30 minutes, until it has a golden top and a toothpick comes out clean. Allow to cool on a rack for 1 hour before unmolding the springform.

2. Make the Rose Sponge Cake.

2A. Preheat the oven to 165°C / 325°F.

2B. Sift the spelt and baking powder in a separate bowl and set aside.

2C. Grease and then line a 10-inch springform pan with parchment.

2D. Cream the butter and sugar together by using a mixer or whisking by hand for 3–5 minutes. You want the creamed butter and sugar to be pale and fluffy.

2E. Add the eggs one at a time, mixing each one in as you go. Scrape down the sides of the bowl after each egg. When all the eggs are added, continue mixing for another minute.

2F. Add the vanilla and rosewater. Mix until well integrated.

2G. Add the flour to your cake batter, mix just until fully combined. Transfer batter into the springform pan and place in preheated oven.

Rose Sponge Cake Ingredients

170 g / scant 1½ cups spelt flour
10 ml / 2 tsp baking powder
170 g / ¾ cup butter,
    room temperature
170 g /¾ cup + 1 Tbsp sugar
3 eggs, room temperature
5 ml / 1 tsp vanilla
5 ml / 1 tsp rosewater

CAKE TIP: Whole-grain baked goods often turn golden or darken in colour quicker than white flour recipes. This means things often appear done but haven't yet reached a fully cooked internal temperature or stabilizing point. Signs to look for that a cake is set: when you shake it, it doesn't wobble in the centre; the cake is pulling away from the sides of the pan; a toothpick insertion comes out clean.

continued...

**Fondant Leaves
Ingredients**
1 cup fondant
green food colouring

2J. Bake for 30–35 minutes, until it has a golden top and a toothpick comes out clean. Allow to cool on a rack for 1 hour before unmolding the springform.

3. While the cakes are baking and/or cooling, make the Fondant Leaves.

3A. Take 1 cup of the fondant and work in a few drops of green food colouring in to create a shade that compliments your green buttercream and reminds you of a leafy green.

3B. Roll out the fondant until it is about ¼ inch thick. With a sharp paring knife, carve out the shape of a leaf either freehand or draw and cut one out on cardboard to make a form or use a cookie cutter. Put aside. Roll out 12–16 long and slender leaves for the iced sides of the nettle base.

ASSEMBLY

For this stage, you don't want the buttercreams to be cold. Remove them from the fridge so they feel workable, and can be spread easily.

1. Place the nettle cake on a serving tray, cake stand, or a springform base so it can be moved later, if needed.

2. Take the green vanilla buttercream and frost the top and sides of the bottom nettle layer. Use the buttercream to smooth and straighten this layer of the cake. *Make sure to save ¾ cup of the green buttercream* to pipe onto the cake seams later.

3. Cut the rose cake across the middle so you have 2 round cake disks. Place 1 layer on top of the iced nettle cake. This will be the bottom of your jam-filled rose cake.

4. Spread the raspberry jam on the top of this sponge layer and then carefully place the remaining cake disk on top of the first one.

5. Take the pink rose buttercream and ice the sides and top of the rose cake tiers. This part takes some precision as you want to avoid getting the pink icing onto the green layer below. *Make sure you leave ¾ cup of the pink buttercream to pipe onto the top of the cake.*

6. Put the pink buttercream into a piping bag with a floral-inspired tip. Pipe and ice the top edge of the rose cake.

7. Dollop and smear a thick circle of raspberry jam about 2–3 inches in diameter onto the very top centre of the cake.

8. Enclose the jam circle by piping a small circle of buttercream rosettes around and right up against the jam circle.

9. Pipe a line of icing around the bottom edge of the rose cake where it meets the nettle cake. Pipe straight and then stop every 2 inches for a rosette and continue this pattern around the whole circumference where the rose cake meets the nettle cake.

10. Take small amounts of the chopped Raisin Caramel Crunch in your hand and gently press the bits against the bottom inch of the nettle cake. You are making a bottom border with the raisin caramel, reminiscent of soil.

11. To finish, apply the varied leaves to the sides of the green cake. Finally, scatter a bit of the slivered raisin caramel on the very top of the cake.

12. If it's rose season and you can forage some wild rose petals, those can also be a finishing decor for the top or pink sides of the rose cake.

Serve and enjoy.

DOUGHBOYS
& MOLASSES

Doughboys are, for me, the most significant ancestral food to my family. Apart from their utter deliciousness and crowd-pleasing nature, they tell a story about a different time in Atlantic Canadian history, of a transition towards eating mostly white flour. They might be called toutons in Newfoundland, bannock or fry bread for some First Nations.

There's a reason for these similarities, as both doughboys and bannock tell a story about the history of grains. They reference an era when local food systems were eradicated through colonization (in the case of Indigenous communities) or they never existed in the first place (in the case of coastal settler colonies) in an increasingly industrialized economy. Doughboys can be traced back to the basic staple breads that were made on boats during the colonial expansion and the slave-trade shipping era. The fact that molasses was a by-product of sugar refineries, often populated by enslaved people or indentured workers, is not lost on me.

Within the span of my grandmother's years, the significance of doughboys changed for her and her community. As a child, either bread or fried dough served with molasses were a daily food for her. For her children and grandchildren, hot bread (either fried or baked) was a common but always savoured treat. The same can be said for many families who transitioned from austere depression and Second World War–era working-class living conditions to middle-class comfort living over the second half of the twentieth century. All the while white flour and monoculture were becoming more culturally entrenched. The fact that molasses consists of most of the nutrients removed from an agricultural product to make white sugar echoes how the bran and germ contain most of the nutrients removed to make white flour.

My mom grew up in Blacks Harbour, New Brunswick, and we would live there together after my parents split up. It's a modest, sturdy fish-processing town on the Bay of Fundy. It's also where my grandmother moved at age twelve with her siblings and mother. They were looking to improve the family conditions; Blacks Harbour featured a movie theatre, but more importantly had a sardine-packing plant at its heart. The plant was built on a harbour that empties out completely at low tide. Sticky, salty, and sometimes deliciously putrid seaweed ocean winds are typical in Blacks Harbour, as is thick fog.

Despite the massive economic changes that happened to much of the Maritimes after the First World War, the fishing industry and sardine factory were still the root of this community for generations. In fact, the factory is still in operation, and the company itself, Connors Brothers, presents itself as the only remaining producer of sardines in North America. Each year, they would host a free fair for their workers and their kin. It had rides, games with prizes, savoury snacks galore, cotton candy, and of course, an annual sardine-packing contest.

I never got to pack sardines for work or for competition, and by the time I was old enough to attend, my grandmother wasn't interested in competing, despite having some skill after years working the factory floor; her packing years were behind her.

Fish-packing included, this Labour Day celebration was a beloved token of appreciation and a good dose of fun. It was a weekend to celebrate the labour of food production, for kids to enjoy the final days of summer heat before the return to class, and the return of the cold, Fundy Bay winds. Each kid attending was given a little booklet of tickets, a joyful stapled cluster of paper tabs with precious offerings on them— ride entrance, game tokens, pop and cotton candy tickets.

One of the few things that patrons had to pay for at the fair was found at the local charity fundraiser: doughboys from the fryer booth. My grandmother Jean was often one of the women behind the counter, heaving crowd-sized batches of airy bread dough. Her touch was light and springy, making it look like the dough was almost jumping right into the hot oil. I can easily picture Nan standing behind the fryer, taking turns with some of the other industrious baker women of Blacks Harbour cutting away rectangles of buoyant, yeasty, ripe dough and gently dropping them into the hot fry oil. The doughboys would come served in a rectangular cardboard tray, the booth featuring a molasses station to serve with them. It was lunch for most of us. Sticky fingers were licked, bellies filled, and many a heart quite plump.

Dulse Doughboys

Makes 10–12 doughboys

Molasses and doughboys were subsistence foods during my Nan Jean's youth. Later on, they came to be the mark of being together as a family, denoting abundance, or at least joyful stability. For me, making doughboys brings me closer to my grandmother, and closer to the feeling of care and community Jean fostered by way of food. I can always turn to this recipe for a soothing, nostalgic comfort food signifying home.

My adaptation of Jean's doughboy recipe pays homage to Charlotte County, where people snack on dulse like chips and you can often find it dried in the snack aisle of local stores.

My version is also made with whole grains, and the finer the whole wheat you use here, the lighter the doughboys are likely to turn out. If you use conventional whole wheat, the textural difference between this version and an all-purpose recipe are negligible. If you're worried about it, you can always sift out the larger particles of the bran.

Doughboys must be eaten with butter or margarine and molasses—at least the first time. But strawberry freezer jam would often make it on to my grandmother's table as a side.

Equipment

optional: bread mixer

medium saucepan for deep
    frying

Ingredients

2 tsp dry active yeast

240ml / 1 cup water (room temp
    or warmer)

dash of sugar

290 g / 2¼ cup whole wheat flour

2 Tbsp dulse flakes (If you can
    only find dulse pieces, you
    can grind them using a spice
    or coffee grinder)

5 g / ¾ tsp salt

30–45 ml / 2–3 Tbsp of
    shortening, margarine,
    or butter

15–30 ml / 1–2 Tbsp water

750–1000 ml oil for frying, such as
    sunflower or canola

1. In a medium–large bowl or the bowl of a stand mixer, mix yeast with 1 cup water and a dash of sugar. Wait 10 minutes to ensure the yeast is active. It should bubble at the top.

2. Add the whole wheat flour, dulse, and ¾ tsp of salt to the bowl. Then add the fat and start mixing—either on medium with a stand mixer or by hand.

3. As each whole-grain flour is unique in how it absorbs water, add spoonfuls of water until your dough feels soft and a bit slack and not stiff and dry. Once you get there, keep mixing until all the water is thoroughly kneaded in. Then let the dough rest for 5–10 minutes.

continued...

4. *If using a mixer,* run it on a medium-low speed for 5 minutes.

If kneading by hand, knead for 10 minutes, taking breaks as needed. When you stop kneading or mixing, the dough should be satiny and smooth, a little elastic too. Cover in a bowl and let rest for 1 hour.

5. Flour your work surface and turn the dough out, degassing and stretching the dough. Leave for 1 more hour. Alternatively, the dough can be placed overnight in the fridge after this stage, covered.

6. In a large saucepan, heat the oil on medium heat. You want to make sure you have roughly 3 inches of oil in the pan to ensure the doughboys can be fully submerged. It takes at least 10 minutes for the oil to heat slowly. To test if ready, drop a small amount of dough into the oil. If it doesn't sizzle, you may need to adjust the heat higher. Be careful to not overheat the oil, or you'll end up with off flavours and a fire hazard.

7. Once the oil is hot enough, tear off a chunk (slightly bigger than a Timbit/approx 50 g) from the main bowl. Round it gently in your hands and then shape and flatten it into a rectangle by tugging at the corners and sides. The flat dough should be fairly even in thickness and about 3 x 4 inches. Carefully submerge it in oil. Cooking time is roughly 2–3 minutes per side. (See Tips on Frying on page 157.)

8. Line a bowl with paper towel to transfer the doughboys into once they come out of the oil. Repeat until dough is gone or your crowd is satiated.

Doughboys are best served hot with molasses and butter or margarine. If you have some leftover dulse, set it aside as a snackable garnish.

TIPS ON FRYING

- It's important for the oil to be maintained at a steady temperature. If the oil is too cold, the doughboys will absorb too much, and if the oil is too hot, they will darken too quickly and the inside may not cook thoroughly.
- Don't overcrowd the pan. Too many doughboys in the oil can cause the temperature to drop. Two is fine, three if your pot can accommodate them comfortably.
- If you enjoy making this, you may want to invest in a deep fryer/candy thermometer. Thankfully they are relatively inexpensive and can be found at most grocers, hardware stores, and kitchen supply stores.
- Leftover fryer oil can be cooled and jarred for later use. The oil will darken over time, but you can reuse doughboy oil a few times at least.
- Any leftover dough can be baked into rolls or a small loaf. My grandmother often budgeted for this, making a double batch with enough dough initially for doughboys and then some for baked bread.

HOME IS
WHERE NAN'S
OVEN IS

Over the course of the pandemic, and even before, I found myself dreaming about visiting my grandparents' old house just outside of Blacks Harbour. I spent a lot of my childhood there, a safe and happy space brimming with baked goods. For a lot of my youth, my mom and I were a single-mother-and-daughter dynamic duo, and my grandparents Jean and Bill really helped make our lives work. Since my mom was a busy nurse, I spent a lot of days, nights, and holidays on the Pennfield Ridge where my grandparents lived. Their home was a constant for us amid our many moves over the years I was in school. When we visited (which was often), we were folded into a bigger family network. The vast work of being a single mum, eased with community.

Jean outlived my grandfather Bill by about two decades and lived into her nineties. Her passing at the end of 2019 came as a bit of a surprise, as we had all pegged Jean as a centenarian. All the same, she was ninety-two and we were able to say goodbye. Jean had lived through most of the twentieth century and perhaps the easiest part of the twenty-first.

Nan's kitchen was always in some state of action. She woke up almost every morning around 4 A.M., four to six hours before me. It wasn't unusual to wake up to fresh bread or muffins, perfectly boiled yet still warm eggs, and a steady flow of orange juice to perk up my not-a-morning-person body. Mom and I weren't the only regular visitors. Located on a busy road, Jean would receive daily drop-ins from one of her hundred or so nieces and nephews and their kids, my second cousins. Nan was always ready

for it, her literal and proverbial cookie jar of love always brimming. Everyone had their favourite recipes, and she knew what they were. I think it was intuitive for Jean to love in this way, to direct her industrious nature into the work of food provider and host. As you read, and hopefully bake, these recipes, you are getting a glimpse into Jean's kitchen on the Ridge.

When we were able to gather to celebrate her life, we sweetly and softly remembered her kitchen, her incredible crowd-feeding skills, and her soft molasses cookies. Each time a second or third cousin or a great niece or nephew came up to me and talked about their love for Jean, I could feel the power of her care within what was once a close-knit but sprawling and religious family. I wasn't expecting it, but I also was not surprised as to how many comments about Jean's kitchen came up during the wake we held for her. To be fair, most of my great-aunts in Jean's generation (I had about twenty) were similarly skilled cooks and bakers, so I didn't really think her home was unique within the family. But it was. Perhaps her professional life as a cook gave her a confidence and power that made her home the destination it was.

Processing the grief of losing my grandmother has been a slow, steady process. Sometimes it happens in my dreams, sometimes in the kitchen or bakery. It is certainly happening in these pages and when I work through her recipes. In my own way, I've taken on Jean's aptitude to be fruitfully distracted in the kitchen. I often struggle to slow down, to stop, to be still, especially when the results of kitchen efforts yield something delicious and joy-inducing.

Soft Vegan Molasses Cookies

Makes 36 cookies

Equipment
whisk or mixer

Ingredients
80 g / ½ cup cornmeal or corn
   flour
240 ml / 1 cup milk (non-dairy if
   you prefer a vegan recipe)
200 g / 1 cup sugar
285 g / 1¼ cup melted margarine
240 ml / 1 cup molasses
10 ml / 2 tsp vanilla
600 g / 5 cups all-purpose flour*
7 g / 1 tsp salt
2 tsp cream of tartar (this
   ingredient is almost
   obsolescent; it can be skipped
   if you don't have it or don't
   bake very often)
20 ml / 4 tsp baking soda
20 ml / 4 tsp ginger
½ tsp allspice
5 ml / 1 tsp cinnamon
½ tsp cloves
flour for dusting rolling surface

When I was nineteen I had my own (shared) kitchen for the first time. This is when I finally started asking Nan to teach me her kitchen ways directly, starting with my favourite: her soft molasses cookie recipe.

These cookies are of the soft, cakey variety. The spice mix is perfect with a substantial amount of ginger, making these cookies even a little bit sharp with heat. This adaptation is vegan, and my Nan's original recipe is nearly vegan, so I felt inspired to take it all the way as I played around with other ingredient substitutions, including the addition of cornmeal. I brought corn into this recipe because of my love of corn and molasses together, adding texture to this cookie. This is a dough that can be made ahead of time and chilled in the fridge for up to 2 days before rolling out. Serve with a glass of milk, if feeling indulgent.

1. To start, soak the cornmeal in half of the milk. Allow to sit for 20–30 minutes before using, to allow the corn to soften.

2. Combine the sugar, margarine, molasses, non-dairy milk, and vanilla in a bowl. Stir this mix until it is well blended and fairly homogenous.

3. In a separate large bowl, combine the rest of the ingredients and whisk.

4. Combine all the ingredients together, and mix with a sturdy spatula or by hand. Once you've created a consistent dough, place it in a covered bowl or closed container and refrigerate for at least 3 hours and up to 2 days.

5. When you are ready to roll out and bake the molasses cookies, take the dough out of the fridge and let it come up to room temperature, for 30 minutes or so.

6. Preheat oven to 175°C / 350°F.

7. Lightly flour a surface and roll half of the dough out to about 1 cm (or ⅓ inch) thick. Cut the dough into circles using a cookie cutter. If you don't have a cookie cutter, a wide-ring mason jar lid or an inverted glass works just as well. Other shaped cookie cutters can be used as well if you prefer. These make great gingerbread people.

8. Bake 12 cookies on a sheet for 12–14 minutes until cooked. These cookies don't change colour much, but they do go from shiny to matte finish as one indicator of doneness.

9. Let cool and store in an air-tight container for 1 week or more.

*NOTE: This recipe is another of my adaptations of Nan's recipes, and as such I kept all-purpose flour as part of that process. However, I would be remiss if I didn't tell you that this recipe would work well with a finely milled or low-protein flour, like Kamut, spring wheats, or other whole grains that are partially sifted at home.

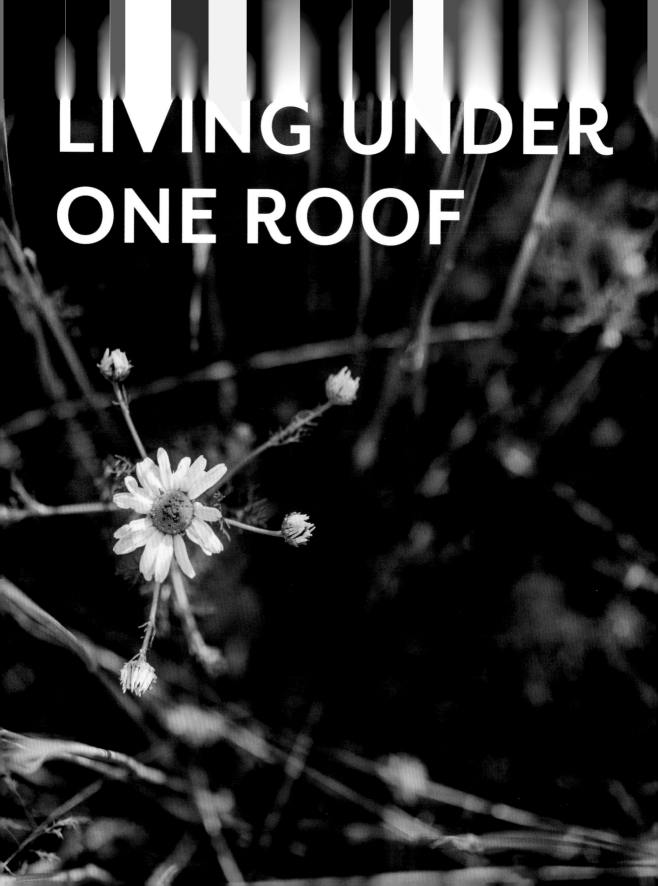

LIVING UNDER ONE ROOF

Summer family gatherings downhome in Seeleys Cove revolved around sweets and treats. The food table was always an anchor for me at family gatherings, where I was surrounded by my many second cousins whom I felt shy around. Social dynamics aside, there were always many different kinds of tender, perfectly baked, fresh fruit pies present. My grandfather's sisters were known for their pie-making skills, among other domestic proficiencies. The Stevens women were local pie pastry masters and Charlotte County is wild blueberry country, so my favourite pie, wild blueberry pie, was a regular star of the dessert table.

After my grandfather Bill's passing in the late nineties, my Nan Jean moved closer to me and my mom, away from her family home on the Pennfield Ridge, the area where so many of our ancestors had lived. Thankfully, we really weren't that far away, only an hour's drive, in Quispamsis. As a unit, Nan, Mum, and I still visited countless extended family members in Pennfield Ridge, where we went beachcombing regularly in the summers and where I would get to plunge in the always cold Bay of Fundy waters. We usually went back to our newer home carrying pies and baked goods of some sort, edible anchors to our home away from home.

Jean's move meant that my mom, grandmother, and I all moved into a house together. Though I missed the Ridge and found it lonelier without my grandfather, the three generations of us living together became a time when my home life felt more normal than it ever had before. It was ideal to have my Nan living downstairs, with me and my mom living upstairs. She had her own kitchen and a new garden to maintain, which kept her as busy as ever. We ate together a lot, Jean always serving something up for dinner. Most nights dessert was involved, keeping her teenage granddaughter soft and well fed.

A few years into living together, when I was sixteen and Nan was seventy-four, she was diagnosed with breast cancer. Her healing involved surgery, radiation, and chemotherapy. This taxed her elderly body and my mom worked hard to care for her own mother, which came naturally to her as a nurse. As treatment rolled on, the situation became critical and our family was strained. It was a tense yet tender time. My grandmother rarely, if ever, asked for help, and I think when Great-Aunt Mae showed up one afternoon to help us, it wasn't because she had been asked. She came for close to a week, ready to provide the special relief women of her generation most often do, care for house and home, support for body and spirit.

When Mae was called to care, there would be pie. Pie for today, tonight, and tomorrow, and of course pie for the freezer. Despite how sick Jean was, we expected her to pull through. All the same, seeing her so weak was hard and there was an energy about the house that Mae's presence offered some relief from.

She also offered to teach me how to make pie.

Mae came prepared to make both sweet and savoury pies, to leave us stocked up with ready-to-go meals in the freezers. Side by side on an early spring Saturday afternoon, she took me through the tricks and trade of making tender, flaky, crispy, and beautiful pie pastry dough. Mae didn't just show me how to make one pie, she showed me how to make a batch of pie crust big enough to make dinner and dessert for now, as well as ready-to-bake freezer pies and leftover pie dough balls for some future unknown fillings. Despite Nan's local notoriety and accolades as a baker, she never made pie. She always declared that she just couldn't make pie pastry and that it was best left to her sisters-in-law, the Stevens women.

Making pie isn't rocket science, but it is nuanced and technique certainly matters, requiring a baker to pay close attention and watch for certain signs. Learning how to make pies alongside industrious Aunt Mae in a time of crisis for our family is one of the oldest baking memories I carry with me, perhaps one of my first ever informal baking lessons. It was probably the first time I was trained by an expert in their field. I've been making pies ever since.

Still, when I make pie dough, whether for myself or others, I gently recall working alongside Aunt Mae, her sweet nature and quick hands. When I cut cold fat into flour, following with a slow drizzle of ice water, just enough to bring the dough together, I'm grateful to have received her lessons and confidence in pie crust. I miss Aunt Mae, but have developed my own industrious capacity for making pies as part of her legacy. I still feel like my pie pastry doesn't live up to the Stevens women's (probably because I'm always experimenting and making substitutions), but then I remember, I am a Stevens woman.

Wild Blueberry Pie

Makes 1 large (10-inch) pie

When I want to conjure the feeling of Charlotte County, I make Wild Blueberry Pie. The landscape of Pennfield, where my grandparents lived during my childhood, was defined by wild blueberry fields, misted by salty winds coming off the Bay of Fundy. McKay's, a famous blueberry farm in the area, operates a legendary pie stand on the side of the old highway between Saint John and St. Stephen. We were regular customers.

I still make an annual pilgrimage for pie purchases and bulk berries for jam making. The style of pie crust that my aunt Mae taught me how to make closely resembles the McKay Wild Blueberry Pies pastry. Using a Whole Grain Pie Pastry crust makes for a more substantive, but excellent pie crust, made for fillings like this.

Make sure your ingredients are cold when you begin, at least the butter and water. If your kitchen is hot, freeze the flour first. Keep in mind that it's easier to overwork pie dough made with shortening than butter. Optionally, you can blend part butter and part shortening into your crust to get the flavour of one and the tender flakiness of the other. Serve this pie on its own or with a dollop of whipped cream, or with ice cream à la mode.

1. Using the pastry from the Whole Grain Pie Pastry recipe (page 88), split the dough in 2, 1 for the top (slightly larger) and 1 for the bottom of the pie (slightly smaller).

2. Mix the ingredients for the filling in a bowl and let stand while you roll out the dough.

3. Preheat the oven to 175°C / 450°F.

continued...

Equipment

Large pie dish (10 inch). If making 2, 9–inch aluminium plate pies—1 ½ times this recipe.
pastry blender or cheese grater if making pastry dough from scratch

Ingredients

Pastry

½ *Whole Grain Pie Pastry Recipe* (see page 88)
flour, for dusting

Filling

700 g / 5 cups of blueberries
150 g / ¾ cup sugar
45 ml / 3 Tbsp cornstarch
15 ml / 1 Tbsp fresh lemon juice

4. Dust your rolling surface and rolling pin with flour. Keep a little bowl or amount of flour on the side to help with sticking as you roll.

Flatten the larger ball onto the work surface with the rolling pin. Re-dust with flour underneath the ball and on top. Then roll it out, continuing to dust very lightly with flour as needed. You can use your pie plate as a guide for how wide to roll the disk. Once large enough to fit in a pie plate, gently lift the dough into the pie plate. If it's fragile, you can gently fold it before lifting it in, then unfold carefully once placed inside the pan.

5. Pour the filling into the pie plate.

6. Roll out the top portion of the dough and lift onto the filled pie plate. Trim the overhanging edges with a knife. Then use a fork or your fingers to pinch the bottom and top pastry crusts along the edge of the pie plate. Poke vent holes in the top crust with a fork.

7. Bake for 15 minutes at 230°C / 450°F then reduce to 175°C / 350°F for another 3–35 minutes, until done.

8. Allow to cool on a rack, serve, and enjoy!

TIP: If you're concerned about the butter or pie filling dripping onto the bottom of your oven while baking, slide a tray under the pan or on a rack below.

SHARING
RECIPES TO
REMEMBER

The Fundy Funeral Home located on the banks of the Magaguadavic River in Saint George, New Brunswick, was a strange yet beautiful place to formally grieve my grandmother, Jean Anne Stevens nee MacGillivray. It was mid-December, which is often an uncomfortably balmy and rainy month these days, but on this day in 2019, though the sky was brilliantly blue, an arctic current brought frigid, icy winds. We weren't sure the ground would be workable enough to dig, and the possibility lingered that Nan's body would spend the winter above ground, frozen.

In the days following her death, I brought out the handwritten recipe book she had gifted me and my cousins some years prior. She had copied out her favourite fifty recipes by hand for each of us. Baking her recipes brought me a bit closer to Jean, her maternal energy something I was reaching for in my initial grief cave. It was purposeful and soothing to be making things to share. I was doing the work, the practice of baking, just like my grandmother, something that now, as a baker and bakery owner, I spend so many living hours working at.

Though she wasn't even gone a week yet, the way Jean had bound us together and what that meant was already becoming clearer. Alongside family fissures that were quickly widening, Nan's recipes were there to support us. At her wake, there were baked goods, and scores of Jean's nieces and nephews, grand nieces, and grand nephews, who came to pay their respects and say goodbye to their aunt or friend, a caregiver. Whether people knew her through family or her work, she was always cooking or baking something.

You wouldn't have known that Jean hadn't lived in Charlotte County for twenty years when she passed. Not from the way her friends and family were able to recall her vibrant Pennfield Ridge kitchen and all the baked goods she would create in it. Nan's home was a hub, a reliable place to go for birthday cakes decorated with boiled icing and candy.

Arranging food for the wake was a space where her immediate family could most easily come together, to provide for the guests who would gather to pay their respects. The food helped the feelings of uncertainty about what the future of our family would look like without the glue of our matriarch. For that weekend, her recipes offered us cohesion.

As relatives and friends came together to say goodbye, we experienced some of those tastes again. My cousin and I had both shown up with homemade baked goods from my grandmother's repertoire. Soft molasses cookies came with me. I knew this recipe would be familiar to most, being both a Maritime favourite and a frequent feature of Jean's cookie jar, in rotation with jam jams, peanut butter, chocolate chip, and sugar cookies.

One of my cousins, an elementary teacher, brought special gluten-free adaptations of Nan's sugar cookies and gumdrop cake, fan favourites. She also showed up with printouts of Nan's recipes, typed up from a recipe book Jean had passed on years back. Many left the wake with copies of her recipes in hand, ready to conjure Jean sometime soon in their own kitchen. Perhaps storing it in their own recipe collections that they may, one day, pass on.

My other cousin travelling from further away had brought the fruit, cheese, and sandwiches to round out our offerings. This glorious food table Nan would have approved of was one of the only ways we were able to come together that week after her passing. I'm grateful we had that, and that I got to taste my cousin's own unique and delicious adaptations of our family recipes. More friends and family came to Jean's somewhat austere funeral than her wake. I understood why: gathering, goodbyes, stories, mingling around the food table.

As both a process of grief and an expression of family joy, I continue to keep her as close as I can and reach for home by making, adapting, and now sharing these recipes. They help me hold space for our family memories. With Nan's recipes, I bring our shared food joy into my present and keep Nan's spirit of abundant care through baking, alive.

Kamut Gumdrop Cake

Makes 1 cake

I n its original (and all-purpose-flour) form, this gumdrop cake was a very popular recipe my grandmother would make at least every Christmas. The listed author on Nan's copy is my great-aunt Mae, the very same woman who taught me how to make pies.

Gumdrops are an old candy, first made around 1800 in North America. Original gumdrop candies were actually spice-flavoured: cloves, anise, wintergreen, allspice, and spearmint. In order to find more authentic gumdrops, you've got to look to the remaining heritage candy makers. Luckily, there is still one of these in Charlotte County.

Even if they are on their way to being as obscure as suet as a baking ingredient, gumdrops can thankfully still be found reliably at bulk stores. For now, Ganong—the oldest operating chocolate and candy company in Canada—makes an annual batch of beautifully coloured and flavoured Gumdrops. (Though I have been known to make this cake with gummy candies such as Swedish berries in a pinch.)

This cake is a joyful one, and is essentially a pound cake recipe, so it is just as good, if not better, in the days after it's made. It has a rich and citrusy flavour, with bright pops of sweet colour, and a cake crumb that stays moist for days and days.

Equipment

fine sieve/cheesecloth

whisk or mixer

bundt or tube pan (you can also use a round cake pan; cooking time may be altered)

Ingredients

225 g / 1¾ cup whole Kamut flour, plus 2 tsp for coating

7 g / 1 tsp salt

1½ tsp baking powder

400 g / 2 cups gumdrop candies (available at most bulk-food stores; Swedish berries and cut up jujubes work too)

227 g / 1 cup butter, room temperature

150 g / ½ cup sugar

4 eggs, room temperature

1 tsp vanilla

180 ml / ¾ cup high-fat greek yogurt (or 240 ml / 1 cup of yogurt—strained for 30 minutes)

¾ cup strained, crushed pineapple (if you buy a can, freeze the other half for your next gumdrop cake!)

1. Mix flour, salt, and baking powder together, using a whisk to remove lumps and aerate the flour mix. Set aside.

2. Take your bundt pan, grease and coat the interior with flour. (*Optional but suggested*: cut out a ring of parchment that will lay just in the flat bottom of the bundt pan.)

3. Toss gumdrops and an additional 2 teaspoons of Kamut flour in a small bowl together to coat. (If using larger candies like jujubes or larger Swedish berries, cut them in half).

4. When you are ready to make the cake batter, preheat the oven to 175°C / 350°F.

5. In a medium-large bowl, cream the butter into the sugar. Add the eggs one at a time.

6. After the sugar, butter, and eggs are well blended, add the vanilla and mix.

7. Add half of the strained pineapple and yogurt to the batter and mix well using a rubber spatula. Use swift, concise hand motions to mix here. Add half the flour mixture, until fully blended. Repeat with the remaining portions.

8. Once the batter is almost fully mixed, take your flour-dusted candies and sieve out any excess flour. Add to your cake batter.

9. Using a spatula, pour the batter into the prepped tube pan and level it off once it's all in.

10. Bake in the oven for 1 hour. The top of the candy cake should be a deep golden hue and a toothpick should come out clean when it is done.

11. Let rest for 15 minutes then invert carefully onto a cake plate or cooling rack. Let cool completely before slicing and storing.

A COLD PLUNGE

CONCLUSION

t's 2016 and I'm driving away from The Kneading Conference in Maine with my baker friend and fellow bakery owner Miriam in my beloved 1980 standard Toyota 2-wheel drive pickup. Fresh off a few days of learning, hands-on workshops, and lots of listening, Miriam and I were buzzing with that post–Kneading Conference glow and excitement about whole grains and the possibilities of baking. We were packing a variety of end-of-conference market loaves and pastries, as well as bags of new whole-grain flours to experiment with. We headed home, north to Charlotte County, New Brunswick.

We stopped overnight in St. Andrews-By-The-Sea, camping out at Qonasqamkuk, the sacred Peskotomuhkati point that I would later return to in contemplation of Nellie and the gifts of the women in my family that would come after her. I loved showing Miriam one of my Charlotte County homes, where my dad is from and where I spent every other weekend with him, my stepmom, and sisters until I was ten.

Each year on my annual pilgrimage home to Charlotte County, there are many stops. A pie pitstop on the side of the highway at McKay's is a guarantee. As is a visit to where my grandparents rest. And so is a swim at the end of the Barr Road, slipping into the Passamaquoddy Bay, on the outskirts of St. Andrews / Qonasqamkuk. Okay, maybe *plunge* is a better word than *swim*. The Bay of Fundy doesn't warm up like the rest of the open Atlantic ocean. It takes childhood (or some kind of adult) bravado to go for it and submerge. This year, I had Miriam with me. She was in.

Unlike some shallow, languid descents into the Bay of Fundy that can take ages, or be futile all together, the end of the Barr Road has a cove with a steep drop-off when the tide is high. Despite it being the August long weekend, the water was still brisk. Unphased, we were bolstered by a summer sun that was beaming hot and bright.

We plunged. A full, suspended, rushing immersion into this buoyant blue salty water, just past the last tide-ring of crispy, sharp black seaweed on the shore.

It was a full baptism for me, a total envelopment by the sea, even if only for a few moments. The cold waters reminded me where and who I was at that moment. My nerves flashing in shock, revealing all of my bodily edges reacting to the cold salty water, the sensors that exist at the threshold of where my body touches the rest of the world. In that cold plunge, I am told I'm alive, that my body is here and that it comes from here.

My relationship to baking is like my relationship with this place. Through baking, I see the connections between place and food, land, and vitality. With annual visits to my settler ancestral homelands, I connect with elements of this place that are integral to my family story. I'm carrying my recipes forth into this brave new world that has such people in it, making my own meaning with them, establishing and re-establishing connection with the places and people who have taught me.

GRAIN
SOURCES

Sourcing whole-grain flours is easier than it ever was before. More and more home bakers are using them, and your choices as a consumer can vary from small independent retailers to large chains across North America.

In this section, you will find regional whole-grain flour producers, millers, and bakers from coast to coast. Many of these selections may be featured at your local farmers' market, food co-op, and bulk store. Even certain bakeries will sell flour that they have milled themselves. If those aren't accessible, major grocery chains all carry a decent selection of whole-grain flours.

This list is by no means exhaustive, and I invite you to find your own sources and establish your own connections with grain producers, millers, and bakers wherever you are.

Enjoy your journey in discovering the actors in your own regional grain economy.

ATLANTIC CANADA

Bear River Farms
Nova Scotian farm, mill, bakery, all in one.
Bear River, NS
902.467.0418
bearriverfarms.org

Birdie's Bread Co.
Nova Scotian bakery with an in-house mill and flour available for sale.
Dartmouth, NS
902.407.0939
birdiesbreadco.com

Balmoral Grist Mill
Nova Scotian stone mill, oat roller, museum, and retailer.
Tatamagouche, NS
902.657.3016
balmoralgristmill.novascotia.ca

Longspell Point Farm
Nova Scotian grain grower, family farm.
Kingsport, NS
902.680.5615
longspellpointfarm.ca

Konrad's Specialty Food and Ingredients
Restaurant supply store that distributes various whole-grain flours to all commercial and individual consumers. They also ship their products across the Maritimes.
Dartmouth, Nova Scotia
902.468.5611
konradsfoodservices.com

Speerville Flour Mill
New Brunswick's best -known stone-ground mill, milling and distributing local grains. Available in retail stores across Atlantic Canada, as well as online.
1.866.277.6371
speervilleflourmill.ca

CENTRAL CANADA

La Milanaise
Quebec mill dealing in both steel- and stone-milling, available across Canada.
Saint-Jean-Sur-Richelieu, QC
450.349.1747
lamilanaise.com

Le Moulin des Cèdres
Montreal-area organic farm and mill.
Les Cèdres, QC
450.453.4559
moulindescedres.com

Graze & Gather
Toronto online farmers' market selling Loonsong Farms grain products.
grazeandgatherfood.ca

Ironwood Organics
Eastern Ontario farm, growing wheat, rye, buckwheat, oats, as well as heritage grains such as Red Fife.
Gananoque, ON
613.484.8709
ironwoodorganics.com

Evelyn's Crackers
Toronto-based whole- grain baker, advocate, and teacher, Dawn Woodward. Her website, The Grain Project, is a great resource for whole-grain lovers.
Toronto, ON
evelynscrackers.com

Brodflour
Urban mill and bakery in downtown Toronto, specializing in stone-milled flours, including heritage grains like einkorn and emmer.
Toronto, ON
416.536.4848
brodflour.com

Almanac Grain
Ottawa bakery and mill, ships flours nationwide, sifted and unsifted.
Gloucester, ON
613.229.1133
almanacgrain.ca

Merrylynd Organics
Organic farm and stone-mill operation, delivering to Peterborough and Greater Toronto Area.
Lakefield, ON
705.750.5837
merrylyndorganics.ca

WESTERN CANADA

Flourist
Bakery and urban mill, sourcing grains directly from farmers throughout the Canada prairies.
Vancouver, BC
778.379.9225
flourist.com

Anita's Organic Mill
Organic BC stone and hammer mill, online retailer, and distributor.
Chilliwack, BC
604.823.5547
anitasorganic.com

Harvest Moon Mills
Stone-milled flour for all occasions. Bread, pastry, durum, and more.
Calgary, AB
403.267.5600
harvestmoonmills.com

Fieldstone Organics
Specializing in ancient grains, legumes, seeds, as well as countertop mills.
Armstrong, BC
250.546.4558
fieldstoneorganics.ca

Tommy's Whole Grain
Vancouvers's first whole-grain bakery, run by Tommy Aird.
Vancouver, BC
778.835.8617
instagram.com/
    tommyswholegrain

UNITED STATES

Maine Grains
Organic stone-ground mill specializing in Maine-grown grains, and host of the annual Kneading Conference.
Skowhegan, ME
207.474.8001
mainegrains.com

Bob's Red Mill Natural Food
Employee-owned international mill, distributed across North America.
Milwaukee, OR
bobsredmill.com

Carolina Ground Flour
North Carolina milling collective, milling bread and pastry flours, rye, and so much more.
Hillsborough, NC
carolinaground.com

King Arthur Baking Company
US legacy mill, active in the use and teaching of whole-grain flours, including baking schools— one in Vermont, and another in Washington.
Norwich, VT
kingarthurbaking.com

Grist and Toll
Los Angeles's first flour mill in almost 100 years, milling wheat, corn, ancient and landrace grains, they supply many of LA's best bakers.
Pasadena, CA
626.441.7400
gristandtoll.com

Northeast Grain Shed Alliance
A coalition of northeastern (North American) grain growers and workers.
northeastgrainshed.com

Bibliography & Suggested Reading

HANDS-ON BAKING

Backen! Das Gelbe Von GU by Christina Geiger (Gräfe und Unzer, 2005)

Backvergnügen wie noch nie by Christian Teubner & Annette Wolter (Gräfe und Unzer, 2008)

A Baker's Year: Twelve Months of Baking and Living the Simple Life at the Smoke Signals Bakery by Tara Jensen (St. Martin's Griffin, 2018)

Bread: A Baker's Book of Techniques and Recipes, Jeffrey Hamelman (John Wiley & Sons, 2004)

The Bread Builders: Hearth Loaves and Masonry Ovens by Alan Scott & Daniel Wing (Chelsea Green Publishing, 1999)

Bread Science: The Chemistry and Craft of Making Bread by Emily Buehler (Two Blue Books, 2006)

Brot im südlichen Tirol by Siegfried W. de Rachewiltz (Arunda, 1993)

The Fresh Loaf. thefreshloaf.com

From the Wood-fired Oven by Richard Miscovich (Chelsea Green Publishing, 2013)

Josey Baker Bread by Josey Baker (Chronicle Books, 2014)

The Laurel's Kitchen Bread Book: A Guide to Whole-Grain Breadmaking by Laurel Robertson, Carol Finders & Bronwyn Godfrey (Random House, 1985)

Martha Stewart's Baking Handbook by Martha Stewart (Clarkson Potter, 2005)

Mother Grains: Recipes for the Grain Revolution by Roxana Jullapat (W. W. Norton, 2021)

The Rye Baker: Classic Breads from Europe and America by Stanley Ginsberg (W. W. Norton, 2016)

Smitten Kitchen. smittenkitchen.com

HISTORY AND CULTURE

Bread on Earth by Living Archive and Research, project by Lexie Smith.
bread-on.earth
@bread_on_earth (Instagram)

Bread for the Road: Intersections of Food and Culture in Newfoundland and Labrador by Diane Tye (Breakwater Books, 2011)

"Cooking As Inquiry: A Method to Stir Up Prevailing Ways of Knowing Food, Body, and Identity" by Jennifer Brady (*International Journal of Qualitative Methods*, 10(4), 2009, 321-334)

Cooking, Eating and Thinking: Transformative Philosophies of Food, edited by Lisa Heldke & Deane W. Curtin (Indiana University Press, 1992)

The Cambridge World History of Food edited by Kenneth F. Kiple & Kriemhild Coneè Ornelas (Cambridge University Press, 2000)

Food Pedagogies edited by Rick Flowers & Elaine Swan (Routledge, 2018)

From Betty Crocker to Feminist Food studies: Critical Perspectives on Women and Food edited by Arlene Voski Avakian & Barbara Haber (University of Massachusetts Press, 2005)

Indigenous Food Systems: Concepts, Cases, and Conversations edited by Priscilla Settee & Shailesh Shukla (Canadian Scholars Press, 2019)

Miijim: Food as Relations. Youtube conversation series (2019–2020)
youtube.com/@findingflowers3227/videos

Pie: A Global History by Janet Clarkson (Reaktion Books, 2009)

Sugarwork: The Gastropoetics of Afro-Asia After the Plantation by Tao Leigh Goffe (University of Illinois Press, 2017)

Sweetness and Power: The Place of Sugar in Modern History by Sidney Mintz (Viking, 1985)

The Taste of Empire: How Britain's Quest for Food Shaped the Modern World by Lizzie Collingham (Basic Books, 2017)

Acknowledgements

I have countless influences in the kitchen. From authors, to bloggers, to friends, colleagues, artists, entrepreneurs, cousins, matriarchs, caterers, and beyond. I believe recipes are archives that hold story, geography, technique, traditions, places, plants, and of course, people. Thanks to everyone who has shared a food lesson or a recipe with me, including but not limited to…

Nikki Auten, Lisa Myers, The Jansens, Blair Marvin, Andrew Heyn, Jude Williams, Lydia Pedri, Richard Miscovich, Doug Brown, Joy Elliott, @breadonearth, @cakes4sport, all of the Great Canadian Baking Challenge contestants, my aunts and cousins, Jeffery Hammelman, Masatoshi Terada, Jennifer Lapidus, Alan Scott, Stu Fleischhaker and Nancy Cantafio, Carole Ferrari, Tara Jensen, Julia Turshen, Bear River Farms, Sean Gallagher, Speerville Mills, Dusty Dowse, EJ Robinson, Julie Lomeda, Amy Halloran, All of the amazing people who tested and strengthened my recipes—Maria Wolter, Kate Day, Ned Zimmerman, Sophie Brauer, Sheila Davis, Natalie Donaher, Hannah Davison, Kate McKenna, Sarah Evans, Timothy Hutchings, Catherine Abreu, Heather Jessop, Monika Landry, Ben Gallagher—Julia Umphenbach, Anna-Sophia Vukovich, Pat Manley, Sandor Katz, Helen Goh, Al Melnyk, Desi Gordon, Joe MacLellan, Jeff McMahon, Katerina Westhaud, Enrique Rosales, Falk Sütfels, Monica from Spain who taught me how to whisk, Sarah Owens, Roxanna Jullapat, Steve McComber, Albie Barden, Amber Lambke, Josey Baker, Dave Miller, bell hooks, Emily Lawrence, Naomi Duguid, Dawn Woodward, Marc-André Cyr, Richard Fung, Priscilla Settee, Stanley Ginsberg, Sidney Mintz, Tao Leigh Goffe, Deborah MacGregor, Lizzie Collingham, Diane Tye, Jennifer Crawford, Stephen Fowler, John Dalton, Jessica Carpinone, Jess Best, Yo Utano, Tomoko Eguchi, Lila Scott, Marion Rose, Rob Shedden, Sara McNeil, Miriam Dennawi, Mac Hassel, Heather Oliviera, Reggie Jordan, Kira Daube, Jen Laughlin.

The grain field photos (featuring various varieties of rye and wheat) were taken at Longspell Point Farm. Thank you so much to the McMahon family for letting us roam and shoot in your fields.

A special thank you to Jennifer Murphy, Simon Thibault, Whitney Moran, and Farida Rady for your patience with me and seeing my vision through. Thank you to Shane Keyu Song for the special grain illustrations Also, thank you to the wider Nimbus team who put this all together and have put their creative talents into making *Rise* the best it can be.

I unequivocally could not have completed this project without so much support from my friends, family, and the Gold Island Bakery team. Thank you for listening to me talk through this project for so many years, for feeding me, and for keeping me dancing along the way.

Index

Numerals in bold refer to recipes.
Numerals in italics refer to images.